Poor Mouse
A Guide to Financial Security

Poor Mouse
A Guide to Financial Security

Dr. Lim Chin Choon

PARTRIDGE

Copyright © 2017 by Dr. Lim Chin Choon.

ISBN: Softcover   978-1-5437-4171-1
         eBook   978-1-5437-4170-4

All rights reserved. No part of this book may be used or reproduced by any means, graphic, electronic, or mechanical, including photocopying, recording, taping or by any information storage retrieval system without the written permission of the author except in the case of brief quotations embodied in critical articles and reviews.

Because of the dynamic nature of the Internet, any web addresses or links contained in this book may have changed since publication and may no longer be valid. The views expressed in this work are solely those of the author and do not necessarily reflect the views of the publisher, and the publisher hereby disclaims any responsibility for them.

Print information available on the last page.

To order additional copies of this book, contact
Toll Free 800 101 2657 (Singapore)
Toll Free 1 800 81 7340 (Malaysia)
orders.singapore@partridgepublishing.com

www.partridgepublishing.com/singapore

Contents

About the Author: Dr Lim Chin Choon:
   Financial Coach vii
Preface ix

Chapter 1	Introduction to Poor Mouse................................	1
Chapter 2	Act Like a Rich Man	5
Chapter 3	Dream of a Better Future	8
Chapter 4	Money and Financial Security	12
Chapter 5	The First Lesson	16
Chapter 6	Learning to Earn	21
Chapter 7	Lecturing	27
Chapter 8	Tuition Classes	31
Chapter 9	Multilevel Marketing	35
Chapter 10	Self-Employed Professionals	39
Chapter 11	Stock Market (Part 1)	43
Chapter 12	Stock Market (Part 2)	48
Chapter 13	Stock Market (Part 3)	53
Chapter 14	Stock Market (Part 4)	64
Chapter 15	Food Consultant	66
Chapter 16	Internet Marketer	70
Chapter 17	Property Investor	73
Chapter 18	Money Exchanger	76

Chapter 19	Trust Fund	78
Chapter 20	Broker	82
Chapter 21	Franchise	85
Chapter 22	Gambling	88
Chapter 23	Plantation	90
Chapter 24	Car Dealer	92
Chapter 25	Collectors' Item	94
Chapter 26	Writer	97
Chapter 27	Artist	99
Chapter 28	Administrator (Manager)	101
Chapter 29	Publisher/Director	103
Chapter 30	Financial Consultant	105
Chapter 31	Rental Businesses	107
Chapter 32	Motivational Speaker	109
Chapter 33	Inventor	113
Chapter 34	Fisheries/Husbandry	116

About the Author

Dr Lim Chin Choon: Financial Coach

Have you ever dreamed of being financially independent? Dr Lim Chin Choon fulfilled that dream. On 31 December 2008, Dr Lim realized that to be independent financially is a matter of choice and not a dream. This wasn't the only time, however, that Dr Lim had reached for the stars and realized his dreams.

Dr Lim was born on 17 October 1977 in Georgetown, Penang, Malaysia, but he grew up in Kuantan, Pahang. There weren't many financial role models for Dr Lim when he was young, but he didn't let that stop him from achieving his goals. He was especially interested in mathematics, economics, and science. Luckily, his parents (Mr Lim Sin Huat and Madam Saw Eng Bee), his fiancé (Ms. Teh Cheah May), his brother (Mr Lim Chin Chuan) and his teacher (Mr Tang Chai) encouraged those interests and nurtured his success.

That encouragement drove him to excellence. He graduated from the University of Malaya (UM) medical school in 2003 and received a master's degree in pharmacology from International Islamic University Malaysia (IIUM) in 2008 and a Ph.D. in Pharmacoeconomics from Universiti Sains Malaysia (USM) in 2015. However, that did not stop him from pursuing even more other avenues of greatness. He has harboured a penchant for business since he was small. After graduating, he honoured his business skills by learning and sharing from the perspective of an investor, lecturer, coach, and mentor.

No obstacle was too great for Dr Lim to overcome! Today he encourages, advises, and guides young people, especially teenagers, to have a good financial head-start in life. His life examples' teaches us to follow our dreams, no matter how great!

Preface

We will always be dreaming of unfound riches and wealth. I am sure each and every one of us have experienced being broke and heavily in debt, one way or another. However, we must always remember that the grace of god is always there with us at our most defining moment – it will either make us or break us.

Financial independence is a decision. By making the decision to become financially independent, we become responsible for gaining our freedom – for not being a slave to money. We instead must become a master to it, in command of our own financial ark through the Ocean of Life.

In *Poor Mouse: A Guide to Financial Freedom*, we see Patrick's encounter with Ben (aka Poor Mouse) – an encounter that will change his life forever. Patrick will go from the "low street" to the "high gear"; he will be transformed from someone like each and every one of us into someone who is totally financially independent – a position that we can (and he could in the distant past) only dream of.

As the saying goes, "Money is the root of all evil." But to be more precise, it's poverty and ignorance of how the mechanisms of money work that are the true roots of all evil."

Chapter 1

Introduction to Poor Mouse

In a humble villa there lived a very poor family by the name of Thames. The Thames family live in a small cottage by the fringe of River Sand. The head of the house was Mr Jacob. He was always trying to give his children the best, but to no avail. The family was so poor that he could only supply the minimum necessities for his wife, Shawna, and his only son, Patrick. Mr Jacob thought that he was destined to be a failure all his life. So he was not motivated in his work. As a result, his work deteriorated as days went by. His boss was not happy with him.

In the wake of 1929, the economy deteriorated, shops were forced to close, and people were out of jobs. Mr Jacob shared the same fate. How devastated he was when he received his last pay cheque. He got so angry that, in order to vent his anger, he scolded his only son. Patrick, in return, kicked his dog, Clark. And Clark snarled at Pussy the cat. And Pussy scratched the church mouse, Ben.

Seeing all the commotion, Patrick began to cry. *"Why I should be poor for the rest of my life and suffer the same fate as my father when I grow up?"* he wondered. Patrick moved to the attic, grumbling about why the rich kept getting richer and the poor kept getting poorer. Suddenly he fell asleep.

Patrick heard a loud noise and then realized that someone was calling his name. He shook himself awake and saw a mouse with a cane. He rubbed his eyes, surprised by the sight and by hearing a mouse talk. The mouse introduced himself as Ben. Ben started consoling Patrick and asked him what the problem was. Patrick explained that he was sad that his family was so poor while others had such a good life. They seemed to have everything but not him.

Ben introduced himself as Ben and told Patrick that he was 102 years old by now. Ben claimed that he had gone through life's ups and downs via trial and error and he believed that he could guide Patrick to riches. However, Patrick had to make a solemn oath that he would follow what Ben taught him.

Patrick agreed.

"The first lesson," Ben told him "is this: Life will give you whatever you ask for, but if you ask for something, you must be willing to pay the price to get it."

"Why?" Patrick asked.

Ben explained that our brain (our subconscious mind) is like a magic lamp. When you make a wish by rubbing on the magic lamp of life, you are sure to get it, if you are willing to work hard after making the wish. "I guess your wish is to be free from the clutches of poverty and to free yourself from the rat race and go to the cheese world," said Ben.

"Those in the rat race," he explained, "are those who are not financially independent or secure – those who do not enjoy freedom."

Patrick asked Ben to explain in simpler English for him.

Ben nodded his head and sat down on a box beside Patrick. "Financial independence means you are in charge of your own finances," he explained. "Financial security is when the money that you receive every month is enough to cover all your bills and expenditures. Freedom, meanwhile, is when you are no longer in need of work to cover your bills and expenditures and are free to roam the world like the grasshopper, enjoying yourself all summer and all winter."

Patrick claimed that the concepts Ben was talking about were quite hard to grasp. He wasn't quite sure at the moment what Ben was trying to explain. "Further, if this is the case, then when can I buy the cars and houses that I see those rich people on the other side of River Sand have?" Patrick asked.

"A house and a car at your tender age would be only a luxury," Ben replied. "You can buy luxury goods when the amount of extra cash that you have is more than ten times the price you pay for the luxury goods."

"I want, I want," Patrick said. "I want to be rich. I want to have cars, houses, and every luxury that money can buy."

"Okay," Ben said. "Thus, your first assignment is to be a rich man. Do you know how to be a rich man?"

"No," Patrick said.

"You must try to act like one. First, learn about the character of a rich man and apply what you've learned in your daily life," Ben told him.

Patrick nodded.

"It's 10 p.m. now, and it's time for me to sleep," Ben added, yawning.

Patrick replied, "Sure my financial guru."

Ben laughed. "Just call me Poor Mouse," he said jokingly, "as it's been my nickname since I was small."

"Poor Mouse – or should I say Ben – when can we meet again?"

"Rich Man, we will meet here every Saturday morning, if that's okay with you," Ben replied, adding, "Make sure you act like a rich man for a week as your assignment."

Patrick nodded and thanked Ben.

Chapter 2

Act Like a Rich Man

The next morning, Patrick came up with a list of characteristics and habits of a rich man.

Patrick's list went as follows:

a) Have a lot of money.
b) Be free from money problems.
c) Shop and eat in expensive places.
d) Buy in cash and not credit.
e) Have no debt.
f) Buy quality goods.
g) Do not gamble
h) Always help the poor. Be a philanthropist, not a miser.
i) Have lots of friends
j) Be good at money management.
k) Be humble.
l) Be willing to learn.
m) Enjoy life.
n) Command respect.
o) Have whatever you want.

p) Be willing to pay a high price for good advice.
q) Don't need to work – have money work for you.
r) Spend thriftily.
s) Be hard-working and versatile.
t) Be good at getting the right opportunity.
u) Know the right time, place, and person.
v) Be happy.
w) Be willing to learn.
x) Have good principles starting at an early age. "You cannot break good principles; you can only break yourself if you go against those principles".
y) Have lots of goals in life.
z) Prioritize good habits – "make a good habit, and the good habit will make you".

Patrick was satisfied with the list, but he seemed not to be able to act like a rich man. Patrick cried because he thought that he was doomed to be a failure; after all, he can write down the characteristics and habits of a rich man, but he could not act like one.

On Saturday morning, Ben was waiting for Patrick at the attic. Ben said, "You must have been crying all day to have such panda eyes."

"Isn't it difficult to be a rich man?" Patrick responded.

"Everyone knows a rich man but not everybody will be rich," Ben told him. "Only the chosen few will be rich"

Patrick nodded in agreement.

"To be rich, one must have a lot of money. And to have lots of money, you must have good principle regarding money," Ben added.

"I will teach you how to make your dream of a better future a reality in the next week," Ben told Patrick. "Ponder on the topic. Try to reach for the stars, so much that, if you don't reach the stars, you will at least reach the moon."

Ben laughed and told Patrick that he had started on the journey to riches.

Chapter 3

Dream of a Better Future

Patrick met Ben again on a Saturday evening in the attic.

Ben challenged Patrick to dream of a better future as if the dream was a reality. Specifically, he was to dream of abundance and avoid having a scarcity mentality.

Patrick asked, "Is there a different between abundance and scarcity mentality?"

Ben answered yes and explained further. "Abundance means there are a lot of things for everyone. Everyone can be rich, and we should wish for our neighbour to prosper. On the other hand, scarcity mentality means everything is limited. If I win, you lose."

Ben explained further that every one of us does not need to become bankrupt before we learn about the law of abundance.

"The law of abundance means that we learn and apply the cycle of earn, save, invest, and protect, whilst we strive for everyday improvement."

Patrick asked Ben to explain further about everyday improvement.

Ben explained that he had learned about the concept of everyday improvement or "kaizen" from his cousin, Alex, who was a successful and rich mouse in Japan. "The concept of kaizen," Ben told him, "means that you are a better person today compared to yesterday and a better person tomorrow compared to today, with a sound believe in yourself based on concept of 'I *can*'."

Patrick pondered for a moment what Ben had said and then asked for a clarification. "Does 'I *can*' means that you are confident and believe in your own capability?" he wanted to know further.

Ben exclaimed that Patrick was absolutely right.

"Ben, you are so knowledgeable," Patrick said.

Ben said that he had learned the hard way by climbing through the rank and file at the University of Hard Knocks, whilst Patrick would learn from his experience on a silver platter.

Patrick wondered how good it would be if the knowledge he was gaining were to be learn and applied by his other friends in school.

Ben asked Patrick whether he knew what he wanted to do with his life.

Patrick said, "No."

Ben said that this meant that he was going into life without a goal and mission. "If you want to be rich, becoming rich should be your goal. And your mission, once you achieve richness should be to become a millionaire."

Patrick asked, "Isn't one million only a number? Why should we be using it as our mission?"

"We need it as a benchmark or mission," Ben answered. "That way, we will know that we are on the right track to reach our goals."

"What about prayers to god so that we reach our goal to be rich as fast as possible?" Patrick asked.

Ben answered, "Sure, we have to have some spiritual support. Remember the axiom man proposes but god disposes."

"If that is the case, I will pray for riches from this very day," Patrick said.

"Excellent!" Ben said. "But you still need the right emotional make-up to be rich."

"How do I get the right emotional make-up?" Patrick asked.

"By writing yourself a million-dollar cheque," Ben replied.

Patrick asked, "Why?"

"If your emotional chemistry is congruent with your goals," Ben explained, "you will achieve your goals more quickly and easily."

Patrick asked Ben to explain further.

"If you are willing to go all out – physically, emotionally, and spirituality – in the pursuit of becoming rich, you will be rich," Ben told him. "Some people want to be rich, but spiritually, they believe that money is the root of all evil. So how can they be on the right direction to be rich? It's like stepping on the accelerator and the brake at the same time while cruising your financial ark to riches. Will the ark move?"

Patrick replied, "Surely no."

Ben asked Patrick to ponder whether he was a slave to money.

"Yes," sent Patrick after moment's thought.

"How?" Ben asked.

Patrick answered quickly. "If I work for money, that means I am a slave to money. If money works for me, I am the master of money."

"Good," Ben said. "You have learned well, my friend."

Patrick questioned his new friend further. "Isn't it better to have riches by way of inheritance?"

"Is it better to get fishes or to learn the skill of fishing?" Ben replied.

"It is better to gain the skill of fishing," Patrick answered. "Then we would be able to fish anywhere anytime."

"Exactly!" Been replied. "If I am to teach you how to fish, I will have fed you for a lifetime. Your duty for this week," he added, "is to learn about the topic 'what is money'."

Patrick and Ben were both tired. Before they parted and went their separate ways to go to bed, they wished each other goodnight.

Chapter 4

Money and Financial Security

This time when Patrick met up again with Ben, he had more questions than answers about money.

To start, Ben asked Patrick, "Do you know what money is and how to make it?"

Patrick answered, "Money is a medium of exchange, where you can exchange it for goods and services."

Ben nodded his head and enquired, "Anything else?"

Patrick thought for a moment. "Money is net worth or, in other words, how much you are worth," he offered hesitantly.

"Explain further," Ben prompted.

"A person with one million dollars is worth monetarily a hundred times more than a person with ten thousand dollars."

Ben enquired further, "What is so important about this piece of paper called money?"

Patrick replied, "Only to buy goods and services I guess."

Ben nodded pensively before prompting, "Or think of this another way. How would you describe the type of life where you are always lacking money?"

"Miserable," Patrick replied.

"Why?" Ben asked.

Patrick explained that, without money, all the good things that you can do for your family or your countrymen are limited. Or in other words, money is a limited commodity.

"What's that?" Ben asked.

Patrick elaborated further, explaining that describing money as a "limited commodity" means that it is a limited resource.

"If money is a limited resource, what should we do with it?" Ben asked.

"Earn it, save it, and invest it," Patrick said.

"Good!" Ben replied. "Then must we be educated about money or, in other words, have knowledge on financial security?"

"Yes," said Patrick, "but it seems not many of my friends are interested in financial security. They claim that money is the root of all evil."

"That's because they don't understand the important of money!" Ben replied. "Imagine that you are a bankruptcy."

"What's that?" Patrick asked.

"It's when a person who cannot honour his or her debt is declared insolvent," Ben explained, adding, "In other words, the person has no more liquid cash."

"Oh that would be awful," Patrick said, sounding dismayed. "They couldn't own anything – no cars, no house and no property."

"In Babylon," Ben explained further, "those who are bankrupt will be sold into slavery. Must we be degraded to such conditions in life when we could have avoided it if we were only to learn about financial security?"

"Definitely no," Patrick replied quickly, "unless you are not sensible enough to think about it."

"So, what is the meaning of the magic phrase *financial security*?" Ben asked. "What is secure?"

"Safe," Patrick said.

"So financial security means you are financially safe," Ben explained. "It means you have more money coming in (your income) than money going out (your expenditures) every month, and you are able to honour your debt and eventually be debt free."

Patrick suggested that one should then increase his or her income and decrease his or her expenditures.

Ben agreed and elucidated that this was the principle of budgeting. The goal was to increase your income, either by your work – this, he explained, was called "active income" – or by using money to get more money, "passive income". Simultaneously, you work to reduce your expenditures by spending only on those things that give you value for the amount of money you're spending. "Don't spend lots of money on doodads," Ben explained further, adding, "and not all that glitters is gold."

Patrick asked for clarification. He wanted to know whether, by doodads, Ben was referring to unnecessary items. "As for 'all that glitters is not gold'," he added, "Do you mean that we must differentiate between good and bad investments?"

Ben nodded with a smile and asked Patrick what he had learned today.

Patrick recapped. "What I have learned today is the value of money, financial security, and budgeting."

"It's getting late," Ben said. "Let me have a rest."

"Okay, master," Patrick replied.

"Do ponder on ways to make money," Ben told him. "This will be very important, as the more ways you know on how to make money – or we can say, the more varied the stream of your income – the faster you will arrive at your citadel of richness. However, richness has to be a perpetual process, as inflation will catch up with what you have."

Patrick asked, "Isn't that the same with the price of sweets? I use to get twenty cents for my pocket money, but sweets were only ten cents for three. Now, my pocket money has increased to thirty cents, but sweets are now thirty cents for four. If we are not ahead of inflation," he added, "we will lose out."

"Yup," Ben agreed.

"Thank you," Patrick said.

"May the passion to be financially secure be with you," Ben replied.

Patrick chuckled. "Goodnight, master Yoda."

Chapter 5

The First Lesson

"Okay," Ben said to start their next meeting, "here is the first lesson on gaining riches. Say, we have two friends, John and Alex. John earns $1.000 a month and spends $1.100 a month, whilst Alex earns $100 a month and spends $50 a month.

"Between John and Alex," Ben asked, "Who is earning more?"

"John," Patrick answered.

Ben asked a further question. "Who is getting richer as days go by, John or Alex?"

"Alex," Patrick answered.

Ben asked "why".

Patrick explained that John was earning more, but he spent more than he got each month. Alex, on the other hand, earned less, but he saved some of his money each month.

"Saving is the way to riches."

"It's like water in the tub," Patrick mused. "At the end of the day, it's not how much water you put in or how much water you take out. What's important is how much water is left."

"Richness is like water, and the tub is like wealth. The more money you put in and the less money you take out, the wealthier you become," Ben confirmed.

Patrick nodded his head. "If this is the case," he said, "I will keep every penny I can find and not spend any."

"That's bad," Ben told him. "After all, money is only a medium of exchange. We want to be rich, but we don't want to end up being a miser. Remember Mr Scrooge in *A Christmas Carol*. Do you want to end up as the richest man in a grave who has lived a miserable life?"

Patrick looked puzzled. "Please advise me further," he said.

"We want to be rich," Ben added, "but at the same time, we want to live a rich and fulfilling life."

"Hmm," Patrick replied.

"Therefore, we must create a system for making money and let the system works for us," Ben continued.

"What's that?" Patrick asked.

Ben explained, "A system is a process of making money that we have created – a process that works for us day in and day out."

Patrick persuaded Ben to guide him further.

"First," Ben told him, "you must make a good and decent earning. Then you pay yourself the first 20 per cent and spend less than the 80 per cent that is left.

"Whether you need it to buy your favourite transformers toys, pizza, or anything else, you must never touch the 20 per cent," Ben added. "That's what we call discipline."

Patrick frowned and replied sulkily, "Like that, I will be constantly losing to Desmond, who has all the best toys and gadgets in town."

"It's this very attitude – this determination not to lose to the Joneses – that traps grown-ups in the working cycle; they earn a lot, spend a lot, collect debt each month, and live in fear of becoming broke if they don't receive their pay cheques on time."

"My earning were so small," Patrick pressed. "How can I become wealthy I earn only a hundred dollars a month. If, I save say fifty dollars a month, I will have six hundred dollars in a year. But to be a millionaire, I would have to save for more than 1.5 years. Going on like that, I will never be rich. In the end, for me, being rich is only a dream. The only way to riches is to have been born into a rich family."

"This is only partly true," Ben told him. "Let me proceed by overcoming all your doubts and assumptions.

"Your first assumption is that your amount of savings per year is small. This assumption is wrong because the money that you save can be invested to earn more money for you each year, and compounding the money each year will make you very rich."

Patrick perked back up. "Please explain further, my good friend," he said eagerly.

Ben smiled. "Let's say Cheese Island is an island free of mice. However, a pair of mice, Jack and Jill, comes to Cheese Island and decides to start a family. In the first year, Jill gives birth to eight, or four pair of, little mice, and Cheese Island can maintain a population of a million mice. How long will it take for Cheese Island to be populated by mice?" He paused a moment and then answered his own question. "It takes only ten years for the mouse population to reach more than one million. So, you see! The magic of compounding will make you rich.

"Your second assumption," Ben continued, "is that the way to riches is only a dream. Everything starts with a dream, but you must make your dream a reality."

"How can I make it so, my good friend?" Patrick enquired.

Ben answered, "Simple, by building a castle in the air. But you must make sure your castle has legs or a strong foundation. In other words, make a plan to be rich, just like Walt Disney did with my cousin Mickey Mouse."

"I thought Mickey Mouse was a fairy tale," Patrick said.

"Isn't becoming a millionaire also a fairy tale for many?" Ben replied.

Patrick nodded thoughtfully. "Yeah," he agreed, "you are right." He yawned. "Anything else master?"

"Your last assumption," Ben told him, "was that, to be rich, you must have a rich family, a good education, or the right connection. This is only partially true. As you can see, there are many rich and able youth who end up spending their life miserably. They fill their days with drugs, alcohol, or gambling and become broke as a result."

"So, what do we need to be rich?" Patrick prompted.

Ben smiled. "We need a good attitude, strong desire, discipline, a strategy, and a plan to be rich."

"Yes, master Yoda," Patrick replied.

"You are getting sleepy," said Ben, "and today's discussion has left you with a lot to ponder. Please try to list multiple streams of income that will lead you to richness. Get a good night sleep and think with a clear mind tomorrow."

Patrick nodded. "Goodbye, Ben," he said.

Let us leave both of our friends as they lie in their beds and dream of a better future and start dreaming of a better future for ourselves.

Chapter 6

Learning to Earn

It had been a bright, sunny day, and as usual, a cold breeze had come in the evening. Patrick and Ben were discussing the right path to financial wealth.

Ben asked Patrick whether he has pondered the various streams of income or careers that enabled people to earn money. Patrick answered "yes" and showed Ben the list he'd compiled.

Ben glanced down the list, which read:

1) Lecturer/educator
2) Tuition teacher/tutor
3) Multilevel marketer
4) Retail shop owner (of a pharmacy or clinic)
5) Stock market investor
6) Food consultant (hawker, or recipe proprietor)
7) Internet (eBay, Lelong, own website)
8) Property
9) Money exchanger (PayPal, world currency)
10) Trust funds (ASB, ASN, bonds, REITs)
11) Fund manager or insurance agent

12) Franchise owner (KFC, McDonald's)
13) Investment certificates (T-Bonds and government securities, as well as other bonds, such as those from Bank Simpanan)
14) Plantations (rubber, palm oil)
15) Car dealer
16) Broker (stock market, matchmaker)
17) Collector (arts, stamps, coins, watches, amulets)
18) Author/writer (fairy tales, love stories, health or wealth writer, scary stories, comics)
19) Artist (musician, composer, actor, artist)
20) Administrator (manager)
21) Film-maker (like Steven Spielberg)
22) Financial consultant (basic accountant, actuary)
23) Hospitality services (hotel, service apartment, homestay, car rental)
24) Motivational guru (success by attitude, success forever)
25) Inventor (toys like MASK or Smurfs; health food; or miscellaneous items, such as a stapler or liquid paper)
26) Procurer and seller of seafood (Fish, crab, prawns, sea cucumbers, octopuses)
27) Jewellery (crystal, gold, pearls, diamonds)
28) Recycling business (paper, steel, bottles, plastic)
29) Advertiser
30) Publisher (Poor Man Publishing House)

Ben gave Patrick the thumbs up and asked whether he knew which of the multiple streams of income were most suitable to him. Patrick looked surprise and answered no.

Ben said that, in the following weeks, he would discuss the various streams of income with Patrick, and they would choose the stream of income that would be most suitable for Patrick.

Patrick asked, "What should I base my decision on? And How should I determine which stream of incomes are most suitable for me?"

Ben laughed and said that Patrick should investigate and evaluate each stream of income and see which one was most suitable for him.

Patrick looked puzzled. "How?" he asked.

Ben replied that he would give Patrick a list of criteria for investigating and evaluating each income stream. The list included:

1) Reward
2) Risk
3) Basic requirements
4) Advanced requirements
5) Qualifications
6) Knowledge
7) Experience
8) Time
9) Resources
10) Armageddon (putting everything at stake)
11) Maximum return (realistically)

12) Do you have the make up to be successful in this field?
13) SITUATIONAL analysis: whereby you take advantage of the current situation and environment and adapt it to your advantage. Like what Charles Darwin always said "Survival of the most adaptable."
14) Poor Mouse's advice

Patrick asked Ben, "If there are so many ways to make money, why aren't our countrymen rich?"

"Because of Parieto's law, Excuse law, and Parkinson's law," Ben answered cryptically.

"What are those?" Patrick asked.

Ben explained that Parieto's law states that 20 per cent of people will enjoy 80 per cent of the wealth because the poor kept doing the same thing over and over and expecting to be rich. This, he said, that was Einstein's description of insanity – continuing to do the same thing and expecting different results.

Excuse law holds that everyone will always come up with an excuse not to act. Everybody is hoping that somebody else will do what needs to be done. Somebody is thinking that anybody could do it. In the end, nobody does, and as a result, nobody becomes rich.

Parkinson law, on the other hand, says that expenditures will catch up with income, due to people's desire to continually catch up with the Joneses.

Ben asked Patrick, "If I were to give you either wealth or knowledge as a resource to use along your journey to the citadel of wealth, which one would you choose?"

Patrick answered, "Both. What is wealth without knowledge or knowledge without wealth?"

Ben answered, "Most of the time, life is unfair, and we get only one tiny portion of wealth or knowledge on the first step of our journey of a thousand miles to the citadel of wealth."

"If that is the case," Patrick decided, "I will choose wealth."

Ben smiled, and Patrick knew he had made the wrong choice.

Ben asked Patrick, "If there are two men, a rich man and a poor man who becomes rich, which one is better?"

Patrick answered right away, "A poor man who becomes rich because he has the magical lamp to riches. He can become rich again even if he loses all his wealth. Take Soichri Honda as an example."

"Is knowledge your choice now?" Ben asked. "Knowledge is the king now in this information age. In other words, we need a knowledge-based economy in order to increase the capability of our human capital."

"What is human capital?" Patrick asked.

"Human capital is the combination of knowledge and skill a person has that cannot be replaced easily by another person or computers," Ben explained. He added that, after reaching the citadel of financial security, one should rely on the magic of compounding money. "The principle of compounding must work for us in order to reach financial wealth," he told Patrick. "When we reach this point, I believe we will, at the same time, have excessive wealth, knowledge, experience, and time. Once all four are in place, your castle will have a solid foundation, and you can start building a bigger castle."

Patrick smiled and said that it all started with a dream – just as Martin Luther King had always believed in.

"Yes," Ben agreed, "but please remembers about the legs or foundations for success. Make sure that anything you plan to do in your efforts to gain financial wealth is coherent with your goals, mission, vision, objective, and belief system, and most importantly, be sure that your endeavours are founded on good principle and a passion for life. A life without passion is not a live worth living."

"First develop a good principle and have a strong passion for financial wealth, and for the rest of your life, financial wealth will take care of you," Patrick surmised.

"If you are more passionate than the average man, then you will be repaid substantially," Ben confirmed. "In the world of the blind man – a man without passion – the one-eyed jack is king." and he added, "don't work hard towards financial wealth, but be passionate, and financial wealth will be yours for the taking."

Patrick answered, "Yup! But it's getting late. Should we meet again next week?"

"Yes!" Ben replied enthusiastically. "Please study lecturing as a stream of income. Goodnight and sweet dreams."

"Sweet dreams," Patrick called as they parted ways, each retiring to his own bed.

Ben lay on his bed pondering how good it would have been if he'd had this knowledge when he was strong, young, and agile. By now, he would have carved himself a better slice of cheese in life.

Chapter 7

Lecturing

Patrick met Ben again in the attic the following week. Ben handed Patrick a single stick and a bundle of sticks and instructed him to break both respectively. After Patrick had attempted to comply with the request, Ben asked which was more difficult to break – a stick or a bundle of sticks. Patrick claimed that a bundle of sticks was more difficult to break. "It's the same with income streams," Ben explained. "The greater the number of income streams you have, the better."

Patrick nodded in agreement.

Ben said that it was time to learn about the first stream of income Patrick had listed, which was to become a teacher or a lecturer. Ben noted that teaching was a noble profession, as a teacher teaches his or her students to be a better person and, at the same time, earn a decent salary.

"That and the more you teach, the better you become in a certain subject," Patrick added.

"Yes," Ben agreed. He asked Patrick to list other advantages of becoming a teacher.

Patrick said that teachers had flexible working time periods, teaching didn't require a large amount of materials (primarily one needed to be qualified) and teaching was a good option for beginners. It was a way to earn income by selling saliva, he concluded.

"Teachers earn a little more slowly than do businessmen," noted Ben. "But it is a good start. As a teacher saving money, can be slow but steady like a tortoise. However, small drops after small drops make a mighty ocean."

Ben asked next about the risks involved in becoming a teacher.

"There's the lack of freedom compared to owning a business," Patrick quipped. "And teachers are slow to accumulate wealth, especially if their monthly pay is low. Add to that the long durations of study and high qualifications needed. Plus, teachers are answerable to superiors, parents, and students."

Ben added, "To be a lecturer, you need to have at least a basic degree and often a master's degree or even PhD will be required. To earn these degrees, you will toil for many years following the beginning of your schooling at six years old. One who wants to be hired must be academically oriented and able to teach whilst, at the same time, handling students' problems. A lecturer must also guide students to the right career paths. Other than that, you have to choose to lecture in a field that you are interested in, for example, medicine, business, art, accountancy, or computers."

"Is the study period long?" Patrick asked.

"Yes," Ben told him. "You'll need to get your GCE O level at fifteen, your GCE A level at seventeen, a diploma at nineteen, and a degree somewhere around age twenty-two to twenty-five. From there, you'll get a master's degree at around twenty-seven and a PhD at thirty. Therefore, to pursue this route, you must be dedicated academically."

Patrick asked a further question. "Are there any scholarships available for such studies?"

Ben told him that there was. "If you do well on exams," he added. "Certain scholarships will enable you to study either locally or abroad."

"Good," Patrick said and added further that his studies showed that a lecturer had a stable income, commanded respect, was able to contribute to society, and would be able to guide the next generation towards a better future.

Ben agreed and added that teaching was a satisfying profession in general.

Patrick asked how long it would take someone who chose lecturing as a profession to become wealthy, based on both minimum and maximum scenarios.

Ben explained that, based on a minimum scenario, a teacher should be able to save $1.000 a month. By saving this amount for twelve months a year at twenty-five years ($1.000 x 12 x 25), a teacher would have $300,000 in principle by the time he or she retired. But, he added, if the teacher was to earn 5 per cent interest on income with a dilution of, say, two times on annuity, his or her money would double in, say, twenty-eight years. The calculation he used was (72 x 2)/5. Therefore, the teacher would retire with around $600,000 as a wealth nest.

Patrick said that the figures demonstrated the importance of having multiple streams of income in order to be rich.

Ben then laid out the "maximum scenario," explaining that a teacher should be able to save $5.000 a month. A teacher who did so would have, according to the calculation he had explained earlier ($5.000 x 12 x 25) $1,500,000 in principle by the time he or she retired. If that same teacher earned 5 per cent interest on income with a dilution of two times on annuity, his or her money would have doubled in twenty-eight years; again he used the same calculation of (72 x 2)/5. Therefore, the teacher would retire with around $3,000,000 as a wealth nest.

"Wow!" Patrick said. "Figuring it that way, it takes twenty-five years to make three million. Inflation would then dilute the buying power and a person might not be better off twenty-five years later than he or she is now.

Ben nodded and reaffirmed the need for multiple streams of income, with a minimum of one full-time income to sustain your daily needs and a part-time income as a source of investment along the path towards your citadel of wealth.

When Patrick started to yawn, Ben suggested that its' time to say goodbye. He asked Patrick to think about tuition and becoming a part-time lecturer as his next assignment.

Patrick nodded, and the two said good night before heading off to their cosy beds and falling fast asleep.

Chapter 8

Tuition Classes

The following week, Ben and Patrick met again in the attic. Ben asked Patrick whether he had been to any tuition classes. Patrick said that he had. Ben enquired further, asking, "What is the duty of a tuition teacher?"

"It's the same as that of a school teacher," Patrick replied, "only the class is shorter and more interesting. There are more exercises to do, and the student pays the teacher at the end of the month."

Ben gave him the thumbs up of approval. "What are the advantages of becoming a tuition teacher?" he pressed.

Patrick told Ben that a tuition teacher could be his or her own boss, had a more flexible schedule and shorter working time than did a traditional teacher, and earned a higher income. He said that it was a career suitable for those who favoured work that commensurate with income, noting that it afforded someone the opportunity to have a business with a low cost to open and maintain. "And," he added, "A tuition teacher can help our society by training our future generation."

"You have told me the good news about becoming a tuition teacher," Ben said. "What about the risks of becoming one?"

Patrick paused. "I guess I have not thought about it yet," he finally replied.

"Let me explained then," Ben said. "Tuition teachers can lack students or have students who are difficult to handle, who lack motivational, or who want spot exam questions only. They can experience difficulty collecting monthly payments. The work requires discipline and high morale. There are risks associated with business management. Being a tuition teacher requires hard work at the start. One needs to find a strategic place to do business. It can be difficult to get good teachers if you are working with others, and tuition is mostly generated by self-employment or through a family business."

Patrick said that he thought a career in tutoring looks interesting. "I like to teach," he said, "but I might be short of the basic requirements to be one."

Ben asked Patrick to tell him some of the requirements to be a tuition teacher.

"A person must like teaching, be willing to think critically, like to take risks, have good public relations skills and have a pleasant personality," Patrick answered. "Plus he has to be willing to sacrifice time and money and work hard to be successful."

"In addition," Ben said, "a good tuition teacher must have the experience and qualified to teach the subject at hand. He or she must procure a suitable location (a proper building) and infrastructure (tables, chairs, and aboard); get approval from local council for a license; have start-up capital; develop a proper syllabus; be an expert in formatting and answering the previous year's exam questions; create advertisements and a strategy for promoting the classes and able to attract potential students. For the classroom, the teacher has to have proper textbooks, workbooks, notes, and lecture slides, as well as suitable time for students after class. Plus, he or she must be sure to teach the subject in an interesting way."

"Wow, "Patrick said. "There are so many requirement that I have not thought of."

Ben asked Patrick to be patient and claimed that they had discussed everything about becoming a tuition teacher except the rewards.

Patrick smiled. "Please explain, my dear master," he asked.

Ben explained that a tuition teacher would have an additional source of income, enjoy a better quality of life, have more financial muscle to acquire financial security in a shorter period of time, and have extra to spend on things he or she liked and enjoyed – in short, a better and more respected lifestyle.

Patrick pressed on with his next question, asking whether, "if he were to put everything he had towards becoming a tuition teacher, what the end result would be." Ben said that a tuition teacher, could be rich and successful, but, it would always be a family business, unless the teacher, had an affiliation with other business partner(s) and was listed on the stock market when the business was at its prime period.

Then Patrick asked, "What is the maximum return of a beginner in tuition teaching?"

Ben answered with another calculation. That earning will be twenty students times RM50 times five classes, or RM5.000 (20 x RM50 x 5).

Patrick noted that he had seen tuition teachers giving short courses in hotel ballrooms and that it looked elegant.

"That is part and parcel of becoming a high-calibre teacher," Ben told him.

Patrick asked Ben if he had any advice for those who aspired to become a successful tuition teacher.

"A tuition teacher should work by collecting tiny drops of water that make a mighty ocean of wealth and respect from the community and adhere to the societal responsibility of being a teacher for the future leaders of the country," Ben replied.

Chapter 9

Multilevel Marketing

After Patrick's class, Patrick and Ben met again in the attic. Ben asked Patrick whether he would like to know about a job that would make him an instant millionaire – no qualification required, only a small initial output, and he could continue earning with little effort as time went by.

Patrick smiled. "This must be a scam," he replied. "Only a fool would believe in such a job. A fool and his money are always parted."

Ben explained that MLM, or multilevel marketing, was not a scam. "It is as true as you and me," he assured Patrick. "Other than that, it is a quick method to collect seed money and get to know many friends, as well as offering a source of income for those hard-working and entrepreneurial people with small incomes."

Patrick enquired further. "What exactly is multilevel marketing?" he asked.

"It is a strategy in which members recruit members, and each is paid based on levering and leverage," Ben replied, adding, "Each member works as independent distributor."

Patrick said that he liked leverage because, "As Archimedes put it, 'If you have big enough leverages, you can lift the world.'" He asked Ben which was the best MLM to work in.

"Healthcare," Ben answered, "because one can be both financial and health consultant at the same time."

Patrick exclaimed with a "wow" and asked "if there were any other advantages of MLMs."

"Income from an MLM is usually tax free," Ben told him.

Patrick said that he had seen some marketers who understood the products they were marketing extremely well – "marketers knew how to sell, how to present themselves, and how to properly table-talk about their product and company plan and who understood the needs and wants of potential clients."

"Yup!" Ben exclaimed. "The older generation will be more focused on health, whilst the younger generation will focus on on wealth."

"What is health without wealth and what is wealth without health?" said Patrick.

"I have told you about all the good news," Ben added. "Let me tell you about the bad news now." He stressed that there where many fraudulent companies or "up-lines" making themselves rich while those "down-line" grew poorer. The latter were easily cheated by flight of night company; wherby, those at the lower level of the food chain (pyramid), will get small profits that does not commensurate with lots of work). Some fraudulent company could also cheat the hard-working entrepreneurs out of their commissions. He added that customer complaints related to side effects and loss of product were also of concern, as distributors were liable for suits brought against them.

Patrick said that the dark side looked very scary and asked, "Is there anything else?"

Ben said that he couldn't answer the question off hand. But he added that the end cycle of the product was within two to three years. There was a need to cannibalize the present product, he explained, and if better product came on the market, the product would be obsolete.

Patrick claimed that some of his friends had become enemies with each other and their relatives due to MLMs and they had to garnered bad debt and bad reputations as a result.

Ben added that to work in multilevel marketing, you had to have thick skin, as you would be facing rejection. He noted that, in addition, you would need to follow local regulations.

Patrick said that this looked like problem for those who were doing canvassing but disguise as MLM schemes. Other than that, multilevel marketers needed to work round the clock and had no time with family, leading to financial quarrels and disharmony.

Ben nodded. "A marketer must be able to talk and to sell. He or she must be hard-working and willing to work around the clock and must find a sustainable company with a killer product and good incentives – in other words, a good compensation plan. Plus, having a good sales record would be an added advantage." He added that a good marketer at the top of the pyramid chain could make a million or two in a year and live an easy life after an initial period of hard work. "This looks like a dream come true for those with disadvantaged backgrounds. Furthermore," Ben added, "knowledge on product and skills in the power of persuasion are of upmost importance."

"Is a marketer different from those who work as full-time employees?" Patrick asked.

"Yes," Ben told him. "A marketer is paid on commission only. Marketers have no fixed pay and no employee contributions for when they are old. And when their pyramid chain dries up, their earning will also dry up. However, multilevel marketing is a good start for those who are without a job, education, and experience."

"Do you have any advice for those who want to be a marketer?" Patrick asked.

"Find a good company with a killer product and a good compensation plan, work hard alongside a good mentor, understand product life cycle, be persuasive and smile when you face rejection."

"It took us one afternoon to talk about MLM. I feel like working for one to supplement my present income," Patrick said. "Let me look for one on the Internet."

"Good!" Ben exclaimed. "And may the force be with you."

Patrick and Ben bid each other farewell and promised to meet again next week to discuss becoming a shop owner.

Let's leave them alone and read about them later on, whilst, at the same time, improving our own financial lives.

Chapter 10

Self-Employed Professionals

Patrick ran into Ben after coming home from a dental visit. Patrick complained to Ben that his dentist used to charge RM50 per visit but now was charging RM80 per visit. "This is very unfair," Patrick claimed, pointing out that it was especially unfair for his family, who was in the working class, as his father's pay was the same now as it had been before.

Ben said he knew the situation was unfair to the working class. But he prompted Patrick to think how good it would be if Patrick were the dentist (an example of a self-employed professional). "In other words," he said, "switch the stake from giver to receiver."

Patrick smiled and said that, as time went by, the dentist (or any other such professional) could charge more to keep ahead of inflation.

Ben asked Patrick whether he wanted to know more about the rewards of becoming a self-employed professional.

Patrick nodded in agreement.

"As a professional," Ben told him, "you can be your own boss. You'll be respected by the community. Your results will be commensurate with your work, and you'll have the potential of earning a high income. You'll be able to help the poor and needy. You'll have personal satisfaction, along with the potential to own a family business, spend pre-tax money, and proper budgetting on money."

"This all sounds good," Patrick said, "but there are sure to be some disadvantages of becoming a self-employed professional." He was thinking of the previous week's discussion on the MLM profession. He added that, for someone like a dentist who was self-employed, earnings could go do down for reasons completely outside of the person's control. For example, for the dentist, when there were fewer patients, his earnings would become smaller. Plus, a self-employed professional, it seemed, may have to work around the clock for long, busy hours, having little time for his family. (The dentist's son was always complaining to Patrick that his father seldom spent time with his family.)

Ben said that there were other disadvantages to being self-employed, including the need for specialized training; the number of years and amount of money required to be qualified, which could be tiring; and the need to keep one's own accounting. He added that succeeding in such a vocation required finding a good location, fostering the ability to handle difficult customers, working to gain a good reputation, coming up with the high start-up cash, and making it through the long gestation period (it would take at least three to five years to get regular customers, he explained). Plus, someone who is self-employed would need to get insurance and banking advice, account for the fact that his or her services might not be affordable to the general public, and come up with the funds to pay both overhead and employee salaries at the end of each month.

"Can we talk about becoming a doctor?" Patrick asked. "Most of my friends want to become a doctor. Can I become one?"

"Sure you can," Ben said, "if you have a medical degree. You'll also need to be knowledgeable and to develop the ability to have good relations with patients. You'll need to be tactful in handling patients and to provide cost-effective treatment, and getting a good reputation will be important.

Patrick asked Ben how to get good reputation.

"You can get a good reputation by becoming an effective doctor when serving compulsory government service or working for others in the clinics or hospitals," Ben told him.

"What about becoming a specialist?" Patrick asked. "Is that a very difficult and long process?

"You will need to be willing to invest in a long period of study. You'll likely graduate with a medical degree around twenty-four years of age. After that, you'll need to complete four years of compulsory service and four years of specialist study, making you a specialist at age thirty-two. Other than that," Ben added, "you'll need to work forty-eight hours at a time on alternating schedule and the able to handle stressful situations and do emergency procedures 'ad hoc'."

"If it's like that, why are so many people still interested in becoming a doctor?" Patrick wanted to know.

"The money, I guess," Ben replied. He suggested that a typical doctor might earn, say, RM50 per consult with fifty patients per day. "Guess how much his earning are in twenty years?" Ben asked, his whiskers raised.

Patrick did the math. The calculation, he decided, was RM50 x 50 patients x 30 days x 12 month x 20 years. He came up with the solution – RM18,000,000.

"Imagine earning 18 million cash within twenty years," Ben said. "Is the sacrifice require to become a specialist worthwhile after all?" he enquired.

"Yes," Patrick decided. "But we would have to work hard – like the saying goes 'work like a dog and sleep like a log'. And at the same time, we'd have to be inclined to help the sick and poor, or else we would be unable to last long as doctors."

Ben agreed but added a warning. "We must always be ready for a wellness revolution – a movement towards holistic care (a whole person approach) and a turning towards alternative medicine, such as Ayurvedic treatments and acupuncture, modalities from India and China respectively. And we must be true to the call of the medical profession – to help the poor, the hungry, the destitute, and the sick."

Patrick said that a doctor was a noble profession and that he wanted to be one. Patrick bid Ben farewell, as it was time for lunch. Ben asked Patrick to give him some cheese after lunch as a gift for his well-sought advice.

Chapter 11

Stock Market (Part 1)

Patrick sought out Ben in the attic one afternoon after seeing his father complaining that he should have bought a certain stock last week. Upon greeting Ben, Patrick complained about his father's agony.

Ben answered that the stock market was a rich man's game – one that only the rich, influential, and witty could win.

"If that's true," Patrick asked, "why do people like my father still like to dabble in the stock market when outright they know they cannot compare with the big boys."

Ben answered, "Greed and the desire to make fast bucks."

"Is it worthwhile for a poor guy like me to invest in the stock market?" Patrick asked.

"Yes," Ben told him, "if you invest and don't gamble in the stock market."

"What!" Patrick replied with a gasp. "There are people who gamble in the stock market?"

Ben assured him that there were. "Gambling methods include contra gambling, margin gambling and buying on rumours," he explained. "Contra gambling means you buy more than you can afford, with the aim of selling in a few days for a fat profit. Margin gambling means you buy using other people's money. And buying on rumours means buying when you hear someone talking about the stock without checking the fundamentals (such as the value of the company) and thinking that everything that glitters is gold."

"This is the first time I've heard that people gamble on the stock market," Patrick said.

"Yup!" Ben answered. "Such gamblers leave their money to chance and to the manipulation of scam operators, where the odds are always stacked against them."

"When you say scam," Patrick answered, "are you saying that there are people out there looking for prey to make themselves rich?"

"Yes," Ben answered. "They are the fund managers, the pool operators, and syndicates. And they're all hoping to find fools who are willing to part with their hard-earned money."

"If that is the case, why do people still invest in the stock market?" Patrick wanted to know.

Ben explained that the stock market was a place where someone could earn a quick profit, virtually tax free. It could be a place of "winning" for the most adaptable and witty and was the fastest way to collect passive income via good dividend. "Knowing about the stock market could teach you the basics of doing business," he added. "It could make you prudent and teach you to differentiate between good and bad business, as the stock of a good company is as good as liquid cash. It gives you the ability to earn extra income, as a perk when your investments are successful. It teaches you to be alert, to goings-on in the business world and the world at large. It offers higher reward and higher risk, as well as the thrill of being in the game. Plus, it's something you can start, with a small amount of seed money, and it can enable you, to be part owner, of a good and successful company."

Patrick replied in amusement, "That's why so many adults, are affected by the stock market like my father." He added, "Do you have any advice for beginners in the stock market?"

"Yes," Ben answered. "In order to be an investor, you must be able to shoulder the responsibility (be your own boss). And you must not trust anybody, especially fund managers and papers, with your money, or else eventually you will suffer big losses later on when your investments turn sour. Other than that, the market – reflected in the prices – will know the news first and react to it, whether it's good or bad, by going up or falling respectively, and it will do so ahead of the news. Therefore, you must know the market's "heartbeat" and "breath" very well.

Patrick interrupted. "It sounds like you're saying we must act like doctors," he said.

"Yes!" Ben answered. "*Heartbeat* refers to stock price, and *breath* refers to the volume of a stock. If the price of a stock with a large volume drops, this means syndicates are selling on potential bad news, and it is the time to run. On the other hand, the price of a stock with a large volume going up, means that syndicates are buying on potential good news, and it's time to collect."

Patrick asked whether "the management of the company is important."

Ben assured him that it was but added, "A good manager in a bad company will still suffer, as the latter will always maintain the status quo. Therefore, it's important to remember that a bad company will always be bad, even if you have Warren Buffet or George Soros to manage it, unless the business goes through a 180-degree revamp and enters new industries. Take Polaroid as an example. No one can save the company from becoming bankrupt if it sticks with its old way of selling obsolete instant photos, given the age of digital cameras. In other words, a wolf is a wolf even if it is wearing a goat skin. Don't be fooled by a wolf in disguise like Little Red Riding Hood was."

"If that's the case, why do people still buy stock in bad companies?" Patrick asked.

Ben explained that it was "greed to the first degree" that made that happen. "People are thinking of making a big profit with a low investment, without realizing that the higher the profit, the higher the risk and that, if making money was so easy, everyone would be a millionaire by now."

"Agreed," Patrick answered.

"The syndicate knows about people's greed by studying behaviour of participants on the stock market," Ben added, "and fuels their greed by giving out perks and setting booby traps on penny stock. Such stock will eventually make small investors like us poorer and the syndicate richer. We are like the donkey chasing after the carrot while losing the cart that we carry behind us. We thought that we would get a bargain by buying a favourite stock that went up (let's call this voting for stock). But we were being shortsighted and forgot about the good fundamental stock (this, we'll call weighing stock). For the short term, the stock market acts like a voting machine, whilst, in the long term, the stock market acts like a scale, with history to be used as a guide."

"What a blunder people make," Patrick observed.

Ben said that there was still another bigger blunder to tell him about. "People buy stock by looking at past stock price (looking backward) and not projecting future stock prices (looking forward)," he explained.

Patrick surmised that this was analogous to a person driving a car and always looking behind and not towards what was happening in front, leading to accidents, as well as constant complaints about how good it would be to be able to see at the gyroscope in front (or, in other words, the future).

"The front is always blind to our eyes," Ben answered. "But we can detect it with our radar, like bats, which are born blind. I will guide you to use your available radar as time goes by." He added, "There are still many things that we must discuss before making stock investing one of our main streams of income. We must discuss risk, how to time the market (by timing the time maze), the psychology (behaviour) of investing, types of successful investors, and the requirements to be a successful investor. All this will then activate your radar and make us successful in the art of investing."

Ben asked Patrick to read the daily business paper and tell him next week what he'd found in the paper.

As it was 9 p.m. by now, Patrick bid farewell to Ben, and both retired to bed. We will meet them again next week.

Chapter 12

Stock Market (Part 2)

Patrick met Ben after reading the Saturday business paper. Ben asked what he read on that day. Patrick replied that he had read about company profit increases with new projects and some company's drop in share price.

Ben asked what happened to the company that had experience a drop in its share price. Patrick told him that the company was reporting a loss in share price the day before, and the shareholders lost the money that they'd invest in the stock.

Ben asked, "Is that risky?"

"Very risky," Patrick answered.

"Is driving risky?" Ben pressed.

"Yes," Patrick replied, "for those like me who don't know how to drive."

"It's the same with stock," Ben told him. "Investing in the stock market is very risky for those who don't know how to invest, as they can lose more than everything they have. Other than that, you must be ready for a roller coaster ride. You'll be navigating without any compass to tell you whether you are going north or south. Acts of nature can cause you to lose. A company can go bankrupt anytime or suffer from poor cooperation in its governance or other circumstances that are beyond your control (unless you know the company inside and out)."

Patrick asked why some old-timers still lost, even after investing in the stock market for many years.

"Because they refuse to change and unlearn what is wrong before they learn the right thing," Ben answered. "They follow the herd mentality of average shoppers, buying things that are cheap or on discount without really seeing the quality of the thing that they buy. Or they buy the new hot item regardless of its price and value. That's the weakness of speculators that the syndicate exploits to the maximum.

"Yeah!" Patrick said, glad that he was starting to understand what Ben was telling him. "Plus, I have seen my father selling his shares at a very cheap price when he has a desire or need to use cash for urgent matters, like to repair his car or his house.

"Yes," Ben answered. "And that's why you have sellers even when the price is drastically low. We should use this to our advantage." He added that, in addition, it was important to be aware that, on the stock market, one was subject to high commission fees when trading in small amounts, "stacking our odds to the big boys". He stressed the paramount importance of taking the time to read about the stock you were considering investing in, the economy, and global events. "We must be able to withstand the roller coaster ride of stocks, with its severe euphoria and depression, without losing our head (our sanity) when others are losing theirs."

Patrick added, "Those who have too high margin or leverage will become bankrupt if they invest in stocks like AIG, Lehman Brothers, or Northern Telecom. This is an example of a mistake of the first degree in stock investment. Furthermore," He added, "a stock market player will have his or her stream of dividend income dry up when the general market is bad." Patrick said that "one of his neighbours nearly committed suicide after losing his family and all his wealth in the stock market, whilst, simultaneously being diagnosed with diabetes, hypertension, and depression."

"That's the ugly head of the stock market," Ben said, sounding sombre, "You lose your health, and you lose your family, and you don't have the chance to spend quality time seeing your children growing up." Ben added that he would impart upon Patrick important information on the time maze that he had been talking about. "The stock chart is like stock maze where the maze is based on time," he began. "You must know about primary trends, secondary trends, tertiary trends, and also syndicated trend. The most important is the primary trend because the bull is followed by the bear and vice versa. There will always be, in general, four bearish years followed by two bullish years, with repetition as the cycles goes on.

"It's like when you are rolling a ball down the floor," Patrick suggested. "A dot on the ball will sometimes be at the bottom and sometimes at the top, but it will never stay at either the top or the bottom forever."

Ben nodded in agreement. "In the secondary trend there will be the Christmas rally, the New Year's rally, and the Budget's rally as people's opinion of the stock market change," he added. "The tertiary trend is due to individual stock or theme play on commodities like wood, oil, steel, palm oil, corn, semiconductors, and gloves. In the syndicated trend, there is a play on warrant, penny stock, and hot stocks. Plays on telecommunication and technology stock in 2000 with Amazon are a prime example."

Patrick asked Ben to explain further on "technical and fundamental indicator, like the one he'd heard his father talking to his broker about."

"Ah," Ben answered, "this is the bat's radar – the one that we have in order to see the future. With a technical indicator, you should be buying when the stock is on the way up. Based on a fundamental indicator, though, you should buy when you have good knowledge of the company's product and management and when the company has a high profit (low price to earnings), low gearing (debt minus receivables and goodwill less than 50 per cent of equity), and high dividend. With a good company, we buy when the fundamentals improve and sell when the fundamentals deteriorate. The other way around is a cyclical commodity company, as when the commodity is out of favour, people tend to sell commodity stock, and they tend to buy when the commodity is in demand."

Ben added that, if you let the magic of compounding or the snowball effect work in your favour whilst, at the same time, making monthly investments and dividend reinvestment, you would achieve the citadel of wealth sooner than others.

Patrick asked about the meaning of the magic words – *"compounding, monthly investment,* and *dividend investment."*

"Compounding," Ben explained, "means you let your money multiply by buying growth stock that earns and grows more and more each year. Monthly investment and dividend reinvestment, on the other hand, means we invest a certain amount of money in the stock market every month or every time there is a dividend, respectively, on good bargain, fundamental stock that suffers a temporary setback in price at the moment."

Patrick asked another question. "What is the psychology of investing?"

"You must be able to keep your head while seeing others losing their heads when a stock rises or drop due to greed and fears," Ben answered. "This is a difficult musical chair if you follow the herd, as the last one to sit in the musical chair is the patsy. And if you don't get another patsy to take over from you at the inflated price, you are the patsy."

Patrick smiled at Ben and told him how happy he was to learn so many good things today. Patrick handed Ben a bar of chocolate as a show of gratitude for teaching him. Ben accepted the chocolate happily.

Lets us leave them alone and listen to their conversation the following week.

Chapter 13

Stock Market (Part 3)

Patrick met Ben again in the attic after visiting a stockbroking firm. Patrick asked Ben why people reacted differently to different news and to explain the ups and down of the market. Ben told him that human emotion was responsible for different reactions among different people. "Human emotion or what we call human energy in motion," he said, "can be categorized into different group mimicking the animals in the animal kingdom—for example, lemmings, rabbits, turtles, and vultures. As profit can be made by mimicking the animals respectively, we will refer to lemmings investing, rabbits investing, turtles investing, and vultures investing."

Patrick asked whether there was a general rule in investing that must be adhered to.

"Yes!" Ben answered enthusiastically. "Don't average down (I call this catching a dropping dagger) unless you are sure that doing so is worth the price you'll have to pay for the avalanche that will be coming down. A thing is worth the amount a buyer is willing to pay. And don't be greedy."

Patrick replied, "That's why a lot of people lose their money in the stock market. They cannot break the rules but break themselves for not adhering to the rule."

"Yup," Ben answered and continued. "Lemming investing is based on the herd mentality and can result in a mass suicide of investment. Investors will follow the leader in a herd and be unable to avoid becoming a victim of mass suicide when the price drops! This form of investing is alluring because it can turn in a quick profit. It's driven by greed and practiced by contra and margin players with large amounts of stock purchasing."

Ben added that it is stressful to take care of your stock. "You need correct timing in order to be successful," he said emphatically. "Basically, a smart lemming will have the following characteristics and habits: He or she will buy only when stock is on the way up, make sure that technical aspects show a continuous uptrend and ensure that the momentum of a stock – its breath (volume) and heartbeat (price) – are positive. And a smart lemming will run on the first sign of trouble, following the motto that safety comes first; practice good fundamentals, and pay attention to good sell signals."

"What is a good fundamental stock?" Patrick wanted to know.

Ben answered, "Stock with a debt, goodwill and receivables of less than 50 per cent of shareholder capital, along with an increased profit trend over five years, a PE ratio (that means the price to earnings ratio) of less than ten, negligible or low goodwill and low receivables and inventory (except for a cyclical company storing inventory when the price is cheap)."

"Thank you!" Patrick replied "And what about the sell signals?"

Ben explained that a stock must be sold when it drops more than three ticks or more than 5 per cent of the purchase price, when bad news comes in, or when it drops more than 10 per cent of a recent high."

Patrick asked Ben, "Is this a good way of investing?"

"It depends," Ben answered. "If you are good, disciplined and willing to learn, this will be the fastest way to your citadel of wealth. But at the same time, you can lose a lot if the table is turned against you."

"Of all the investing type you told me about, who wins the race?" Patrick wanted to know.

"Initially the rabbit wins, and eventually the tortoise win," Ben answered. "Why do you think this is?"

"The rabbit was winning but he had an eventual setback when he went for a nap!" Patrick replied.

"Yes!" Ben answered "So, five steps forwards and two steps backwards does not make you a winner compared to those who only move forward inch by inch. If you move a thousand steps forwards with only a step backwards, you will be faster and eventually the winner."

"This means that collecting wealth depends on how many steps you go forwards and how many steps you go backwards," Patrick surmised.

"Yes," Ben answered, "and the time factor is important. The younger you are when you become rich, the better off you will be, when you retire, as money now is worth more than the money you'll have when you retire later on."

Ben proceeded. "There are people who love technologies like the "iPhone" and those who like antiques and collectibles like stamps and coins. It's the same with rabbit investing. There are those who like growth investing and those who like value investing."

"My master," Patrick asked, "can you kindly explain what growth investing is?"

Ben answered, "In growth investing, you must see the potential future growth in EPS (that is, earning per share) for the stock, and price history must not be used in your buying decision.

"Is there any criteria that you must adhere to in growth investing?" Patrick asked.

Ben made a list of the criteria to follow when buying growth stock. It said that you were to buy when the company:

a) Sees a big jump in earning per share (EPS)
b) Enters a new business
c) Purchases another company (economy of scale)
d) Gets a new central distribution centre
e) Gets a new shareholder that adds value to company
f) Secures a big contract
g) Benefits from better government regulation
h) Invests in new technologies
i) Gets new favourable rules
j) Gets new favourable partnerships

k) Undergoes a new favourable takeover
l) Gains promising overseas business
m) Gets new or proven management
n) Becomes or gets a brand name
o) Becomes a tollgate monopoly
p) Has a good track record

"Wow!" Patrick said. "So many new things that I learned today."

"As there are buying criteria for the stock, there must be selling criteria as well," Ben continued. "A stock must be sold when the price drops; when it continuously has a negative EPS; and with presence of bad news or high debt, receivables or inventory. You must also pay attention to when the reason to buy is no longer there. And you must know when hanky-panky business is going on, when there are business irregularities and when bad business policies and changes in government rules and regulation may affect the company."

Patrick asked, "What is value investing then?"

"Cyclical investment or trend investment that is usually bestowed on commodity businesses," Ben answered.

"What is a commodity business?" Patrick asked.

"A business involved in raw materials and manufacturing goods that have no distinct difference in brand name, like rubber, wood, palm oil, oil and gas, property, semiconductors, gloves, steel, shipping, construction and automobiles," Ben explained.

"Cyclical also means up and down, doesn't it?" Patrick asked.

"Yes!" Ben answered.

"What is then the general rule of making a big profit in cyclical investing?"

"Buy when everybody else doesn't want to, during a bust when earning are dropping or negative, with a PE greater than forty or a PE that is negative. And sell when everybody wants to buy during a boom when earnings are very high and the PE is less than ten. Usually in a bust, the price is dirt cheap, and it's damn expensive during a boom. Always be on the lookout for theme play," he added, "and dance to the tune of the theme play when the music starts."

Patrick asked Ben to explain what he meant.

"Theme play," Ben answered, "refers to a continued upwards trend in price across the sector due to favourable factors for the sector or potential increase in EPS, and it can last for periods defined as follows:

a) Ultra-short, less than a day
b) Short mid-term, within three days
c) Mid-term, less than two weeks
d) long term, more than a month

"Usually price will remain stagnant or negative unless the fundamentals change like those that happen to palm oil in the mid-'90s," Ben added.

"Wouldn't it be better if we got a growth stock that showed cyclical potential due to short-term unfavourable outcomes?"

Ben answered, "Yes, if you can spot good branded companies during economy crises – for example, Microsoft, Johnson and Johnson, and Nabisco during the subprime crisis in 2008 – you will be rewarded handsomely. Dividends will increase with price when the economy improves."

"Wow!" Patrick replied. "I would like to be a value investor then!"

"Fishing in troubled water best describes this method of investment," Ben told him. "But there are other better investments that come in slowly and steadily. The return on this is great as well when compounded over time."

"Is that tortoise investment?" Patrick guessed.

"Yes!" Ben answered. "And rule number one is don't ever lose. Rule two is, if you don't agree, please read rule one again. This type of investing is suitable for a pensioner who has lots of money but cannot afford to lose."

"Is the rule also to be proud to be a tortoise?" Patrick enquired.

"Yes!" Ben answered. "But the magic word is *REIT*, which stands for real estate investment trust. This is where a certain prime property is divided into portions and managed by a professional real estate agent."

Patrick asked, "What so magic about the word REIT?"

"We must learn about the advantage of REITs compared to conventional property in order to appreciate the REIT," Ben told him.

With that, he listed the advantages of an REIT. They included:

a) No need to borrow from bank (loan and interest free)
b) No need for a high deposit in order to buy
c) No lawyers' fees
d) No yearly quick rent/assessment
e) No need to collect rental fees from a tenant
f) No need to repair and maintain houses and piping
g) No problem with an absconded or difficult tenant
h) The ability to sell part of your REIT when in need of money
i) The ability to afford to buy a part of a prime property, such as the Golden Triangle in Kuala Lumpur
j) A higher potential of price appreciation due to strategic areas

"This is equally good, but what does the profit picture look like?" Patrick asked.

Ben explained by making another list:

a. REIT gives a dividend of 8 per cent per year
b. It takes (72/8) 9 years for the share to double
c. We invest all earnings for 36 years.
d. 36/9 = 4 cycles
e. The appreciation factor = 4
f. Therefore, after 36 years, our investment of RM10.000 would become RM640.000 (10.000 x 24 x 4)

Patrick said, "It looks great to be a tortoise."

"Yes," Ben answered, "but don't be a terrapin by stepping on unknown territory and risk without knowing what you are subjecting yourself to."

"Vulture investing doesn't sound nice in name," Patrick invested. "I am always afraid of vultures."

"A vulture will always shows its ugly head in times of other people's agony," Ben answered. "In other words, in vulture investing, you buy distressed company and gamble your lot that there are food carcasses left in the distressed company. However, sometimes you can find a diamond in areas others have overlooked. Take, for example, the salad oil crisis and American Express in the 1970s."

"It sounds very dangerous, like the sword of Damocles," noted Patrick, "like you will be sliced if you move wrongly by an inch."

"Yes," Ben answered. "The vulture speculator is always hoping that, by kissing a lot of frogs, he or she will find some who will be great princess. But most of them lose heavily and become potential candidates for bankruptcy." He added, "Most of them bet heavily, hoping for a lucky break. But seldom do I see them live happily ever after. They might win big one day, but their winnings do not measure up to their losses, making them worse off than they were before."

Patrick added, "They also like to average down, buying more and more when prices drop, thinking themselves to be right all the time. I overheard story of participants in the stock market buying more and more, when the prices drop and to lose all in the end."

"You need to do contrary to the vulture to be rich," Ben said, "that is, averaging up."

Ben then proceeded to list the buying and selling indicators for successful vulture investors in warrant, as most successful vultures invested in warrant of good companies. He headed the first list "Buying indicators":

a) When stock is cheap (less than fifty cents or preferably less than twenty cents)
b) During a long trading period (more than five years)
c) Preferably, a good company
d) When there is a low conversion price
e) When the mother share is near conversion price or "in the money"
f) When a big syndicate (the big boys or the government) is behind company
g) When the company is newly listed
h) When the ratio is greater than three and a half times the mother share
i) When warrant moves more than the mother share

Under "Selling indicators", Ben wrote:

a) When the warrant continues to move but not the mother share

b) When the warrant is less than two times the ratio to the mother share (if out of money) or high premium (if in the money)
c) When the warrant becomes stagnant or is dropping

Patrick claimed that he had learned a lot today and told Ben, "I will be a mixture of a growth rabbit, a value rabbit, an REIT tortoise, and a warrant vulture to be rich in the stock market."

Ben answered, "You have learned well my friend."

Patrick asked for permission to leave, as it was getting late. The two bid each other farewell and left for their beds.

Chapter 14

Stock Market (Part 4)

Patrick met Ben again the following week. Patrick asked why the top 20 per cent of people made it big in the stock market, whilst the last 80 per cent would usually lose.

"This is due to Parieto's law," Ben told him. He explained that Parieto's law worked because human beings were emotional beings and sometime did things on impulse, whilst, at the same time, lacking in investment skill.

Patrick thought a minute and then asked. "How can we be in the top twenty – among those who are always successful?"

"That requires excessive time, knowledge, experience, and cash. And the most important factor is patience – or you might say, lack of impulsiveness." Ben added, "In order to gain experience, one must always learn from mistakes. As the saying goes, success is great, but the teacher of success is failure. If you show me a person who does not fail, I will show you a person who does not try. So my advice is for you to learn as much as you can when you fail or are successful during your younger days as this will be the ration from which you draw for the next thirty years of your investing life. Knowledge, for its part, will make you better equipped in the stock market game.

And time allows you to strike when the iron is hot. Cash will be your seed capital on which to build your success. It will be compounded into an oak tree with the passing of time. However, the ability to be patient and do the contrary to the general public is the highest blessing a stock market investor can have. It is imperative that you don't lose your head when everybody else is losing theirs."

Patrick asked whether investing in the stock market was based on luck.

"If the stock market was based on luck and not wit, most investors would be on the street asking for pennies," Ben answered.

Patrick asked about advice for young investors. Ben wrote out a list of qualities a successful investor or advisor must possess:

a) Don't be greedy.
b) Be willing to learn (to get experience) and read far and wide (to get knowledge).
c) Believe in the magic of compounding over time
d) Raise some seed capital and make monthly reinvestments.
e) Be hard-working.
f) Be patient.

"Well written, my master," Patrick said. "Do you have any parting advice before we part for the day?"

Ben answered, "When a rich man meets a wise man, they will always make an exchange – the rich man will become wiser, whilst the wise man will become richer."

Patrick thanked Ben and wished him a goodnight. So let us leave them for the time being.

Chapter 15

Food Consultant

Patrick met Ben again in the attic after spending the day with his family at a McDonald's restaurant. Patrick brought for Ben some French Fries and a Double Cheeseburger. Ben thanked Patrick and asked him what he felt when he saw a McDonald's symbol.

"I get a happy feeling and my mouth waters," Patrick answered. "I think about eating French Fries and burgers and the world-class services of fast food.

"That's how McDonald's makes money," Ben replied, "by selling tasty well-cooked food prepared in an instant."

"I guess the theme for today is making income from the food industry," Patrick said.

Ben nodded his head. "Do you know the reward of making an income in the food industry?"

"Yes!" Patrick answered. "There are lots of delicious and tasty foods to eat! And you can become rich at the same time."

"You can also be your own boss, promote local cuisine, and have a high profit margin," Ben added. "Plus, you can be resistant to inflation and a gloomy economy, while promoting healthy and delicious food for the community. And you'll be able to pass the food business to your descendants."

"What's the risk then?" Patrick asked.

"Few customers, high borrowing for your start-up seed capital for a well-known franchise, and high rental rates in uptown areas," Ben answered. "Plus, it's hard to find experienced cooks and you may well suffer loss of key personnel, especially cooks, to competitors. Other risks of owning a franchise in the food industry include dealing with dishonest or unmotivated workers, long working hours (you'll often be working from dawn till dusk), losses of income when you're on leave and a lack of the retirement contribution you've received if you were working for a company. And you can't forget the need to wash dishes, the threat of theft, the need to acquire permits and follow regulations and the need to contribute to workers' retirement."

Patrick commented on the loss of valuable time spent watching their children grow up faced by many franchise owners. "It seems like this could happen often if they are busy all day and unable to delegate cooking or handling of money to subordinates."

Ben replied, "That's why food consultants are self-employed. The richer they become, the busier they become."

Patrick asked, "What is the basic requirement to be a food consultant?"

Ben answered simply, "Good recipes or a good franchise, along with a good business model."

Patrick asked, "What is a good business model?"

Ben answered, "A good business model means a business that makes the customer thrilled with excitement; it's one everyone is feeling the 'wow factor'. And a good business model allows you to obtain repeat customers, along with a handsome profit."

"What about the food?" Patrick asked. "I guess it has to be delicious, right?"

"Yes!" Ben answered. "But if it's also affordable, hygienic, and healthy at the same time, that would be a wow factor in your cap."

"What are the advance requirements for franchising with a big corporation like McDonald's?"

"Good marketing, sales, and advertisement (brand building)," Ben begin, "plus financial and management teams, where each member feels appreciated, as a family and works towards the common goals, of serving the customer well."

"What about the resources needed for a young entrepreneur as a food consultant?" Patrick asked.

"I would say those include recipes and good management of financial resources, whilst at the same time looking for a good location and proper refurbishment of the outlet."

"What is the maximum advantage for a person who goes all out to be a food consultant?" Patrick pressed.

Ben answered, "You can be an entrepreneur with a listed company and own a brand name and trademark."

"What about newbies like me?" Patrick asked. "There's not much opportunity left, right!"

"Opportunity only comes to those who are prepared to look for one," Ben replied. "Consider Nyonya food, Satay, Arab food, and French cuisine as a start."

Patrick asked, "Then what is your advice for newbies like me then?"

"A good recipe for delicious cheap health food, along with a good business model and a brand name will make your dream of becoming a millionaire via this route a reality in a short span of time," Ben answered.

"Thank you, master," Patrick replied. "And please enjoy your food, or should I say McDonald's."

"Yes!" Ben said. "*McDonald's* is the magic word!"

Patrick asked to take his leave and we will leave Ben savouring the delicious food from McDonald's.

Chapter 16

Internet Marketer

Patrick met Ben on Saturday night after surfing the net. Ben asked Patrick whether he could live without the Internet. Patrick answered no. Ben then asked Patrick whether he knew that a person could actually make money and become rich easily with the coming of the Internet age.

Patrick asked how.

"By selling local product like watches, mouse pads and handicrafts to people around the world via Internet marketing," Ben answered. He mentioned Internet portals like eBay.com, Alibaba Group and Lelong.com and how, for small fees, they allowed marketers to sell their products worldwide.

Patrick asked about the advantages of becoming an Internet marketer.

"The world market is at the touch of a pad," Ben answered. "Costs to sell are low or negligible, as are staff costs. No physical shop is needed. You'll have free time, a high return, and economical shipping chargers. The portals make it easy to match the buyer to the seller. And it's possible to turn a profit by buying in bulk and selling in small amounts."

Patrick asked about the risks.

"The risks are bad and fussy customers, loss of packages, inability to recover payment, high postage costs, high insurance costs, and the potential to get bad remarks from fussy customers," Ben told him.

Patrick proceeded to ask about the basic requirements to be an Internet marketer.

Ben explained that a person interested in becoming an Internet marketer would need to understand the bidding process. In addition, he or she would need to get a quality, high-demand product. Skills in graphic design for advertisements; time to advertise, properly list the product, and to pack and deliver it; and a good relationship with the post office were other requirements. Ben added that the advance requirements included getting a product that was hot and in strong demand at the moment and selling them at a proper place and price with good promotions.

"What advice do you have for young people like me who would like to be an Internet marketer?" Patrick asked.

"Understand the business model," Ben began. "Have a good relationship with the Internet business platform you choose. Be willing to spend time and learn. And get a good supplier, lots of buyers, and a fat margin."

"What is the primary benefit of being an Internet marketer?" Patrick asked.

"You can open your own virtual shop, be your own boss, get a good reputation via hard work, and be on your way to become a multimillionaire," Ben told him.

Patrick asked, "Do you have any parting advice?"

Ben answered, "Internet marketing is the marketing of the future, and the World Wide Web is the marketplace of the future."

Soon after, both of them wished each other a goodnight and went to sleep in their cosy beds.

Chapter 17

Property Investor

Ben met Patrick in the attic every week to discuss how to make money. This week, Patrick was late for his appointment with Ben. Ben was waiting patiently, smoking his pipe and sitting by a bench. When Patrick arrived, Ben asked him why he was late for their usual appointment.

Patrick answered that he had gone with his father to a property road show.

"If this is the case," Ben replied, "we will discuss property as another source of income." He asked Patrick if he knew what was meant by the word *property*.

"Property includes our assets, net worth or valuables," Patrick answered.

"You are right," Ben said, "but property really refers to ownership or something that belongs to you."

"We must have ownership of something that is valuable, right," Patrick said.

Ben answered, "Property will not only be valuable but have value appreciation and be a source of passive income."

"Property will bring both monthly incomes for the short term and price appreciation for the long term," Patrick surmised.

"You are getting better and better in your education on generating income, and I am happy with it," Ben told him.

Patrick smiled.

Ben continued, "Do you know what the three magic words in property investment are?"

"Location, cost, and cash flow," Patrick answered.

"Good," Ben replied. "Good location means you find a prime area where there are lots of buyers. Cost means that you buy at a price that is well below market value. And cash flow means that the property brings you positive income every month after you subtract all your monthly expenses."

Patrick asked, "Why is location important?"

"Imagine, if you will, buying land deep in the forest," Ben answered. "The land might be cheap, but you might not survive to see the price appreciation."

"The demand and the feng shui are also equally important," Patrick said.

Ben answered, "Yes. A low-demand area – like places with bad feng shui in a house, a flyover crossing area, a T-junction, a reputation for being haunted or flood and pollution zones – are sold at very cheap prices."

"What are the basic requirements to be a property consultant?" Patrick asked.

"Learning curve, experience, networking, shrewdness, having a golden touch, being hard-working, and a willingness to work out of the office," Ben replied.

"What about rental?" Patrick asked. "How do we increase the desirability of a rental unit?"

"By decorating and furnishing the house with proper furniture," Ben told him. "Renting it to an expatriate or making it into a home-stay will increase the rental of the house tremendously."

Patrick lamented to Ben. "If we want to become a property investor, we would need lots of money for a house deposit."

"Yes," Ben answered, "but we can always opt for REIT or become a property broker, where we become a matchmaker for buyers and sellers of property."

Patrick asked, "What about price appreciation?"

"Price appreciation of two to five times on a good property investment will make you a millionaire in no time," Ben told him.

Patrick asked, "What is Poor Mouse's advice for young people like me who want to be property brokers."

"Hard work and patience are the keys," Ben answered. "If you look for more than one hundred properties, the law of averages says that one of the properties will make you wealthy, either from cash flow or price appreciations. Those who are not hard-working and enterprising might as well buy REITS – where you get all the benefit minus all the headaches or problems."

Patrick bid farewell to Ben and both of them promised to meet again the following week.

Chapter 18

Money Exchanger

Patrick's family was planning a vacation to Thailand, and they were preparing a list of things that they would need for their visit. Patrick's father said that he would look up at the exchange rate for Thai baht tomorrow. Ben heard what Patrick's father said, so he decided his next discussion with Patrick will be based on how to become a money exchanger.

Patrick met Ben and asked what he would be learning today.

"We will discuss a business where you profit whether people buy or sell," Ben answered.

Patrick was surprised and asked, "Seriously? What type of business is it?"

Ben answered indirectly. "Does your father grumble every time he exchanges his money for foreign currency, when he travels and again when he exchanges the foreign currency for local currency, when he comes back?"

"Yes," Patrick answered, "because money exchanger, sells currency at a higher rate and buys currency at a lower rate than the market value."

"This is because money exchangers, profit mainly from spread or commission," Ben explained. "However, this business is subject to wide fluctuation, with the sudden rise or fall of currency."

"This business should be a complementary income source for someone who is well versed in foreign exchange," Patrick posited.

"Other than that, you can also be feeder for e-currency like PayPal and NXpay."

Patrick enquired further, "What would be the requirements then?"

"Money exchangers need a license. They must be well versed in the Forex market. They must establish good client base, have a multitude of currency available on hand and be good at networking," Ben answered. "Money exchanging also requires a lot of time to monitor the foreign exchange and this business is capital intensive."

"What is in store in the future for newbies like me?" Patrick wanted to know.

Ben answered, "If you put all your heart into being a money exchanger, you can earn a lot of fast bucks. But there's a lot of risk involve. Or, in other word, it's like marriage – in richness and in poorness."

"What is your final advice then?" Patrick asked.

"Money exchanging is only for the strong at heart," Ben replied. "The business of money exchanging is like gambling. It can be good for the short term, but it isn't a good method for obtaining wealth for the long term."

Chapter 19

Trust Fund

Patrick met Ben as usual in the attic. Patrick had learned many ways to get rich, but it seemed that most methods required money and experience to be successful. So Patrick asked Ben, "Is there a business, whereby lazy and inexperienced person can become successful?"

Ben answered, "Yes, we call it the lazy man's guide to stock investing."

"What's that?" Patrick asked.

Ben replied, "Another name for it would be trust fund investment."

"Is looking at the trust funds, like public mutual, prudential, or other funds that are present in *Morning Glory* as a guide to stock investment," Patrick asked.

"Yes!" Ben answered.

"Okay," said Patrick excitedly. "There are so many trust funds to choose from. Which one would be suitable to me?"

"It's not the trust funds that are suitable to you, but, rather, those that are most profitable and conservative and that have good management, that, we're looking for. We don't seek the fund, that will give you a high return today, but one that will pay out largely into the future."

Patrick asked, "Is there any trust fund that guarantees a handsome return?"

"Yes," Ben told him, "government-backed trusts like Amanah Saham Bumiputera, and Amanah Saham Wawasan would be ideal in Malaysia."

Patrick asked, "Why?"

"These trust funds have been paying 8 per cent per year consistently."

"This is a very low rate of return," Patrick ventured. "It would take ten years for my money to double. Is there a trust fund that pays a very high return yearly?"

"Yes," Ben answered, "but with a higher return comes a higher risk. You can make, say, 50 per cent of your capital a year or lose all your capital within the year"

"Yeah, higher the risk, higher the gain," Patrick reply thoughtfully. "So, is there such thing as a hybrid fund that will give you a high earning but also the security of a bond?"

Ben told him that there was indeed. "A hybrid trust fund is one that invests in both shares and bonds," he explained. "If a bond or government security gives you an 8 per cent return and a high-risk fund gives you a 40 per cent return, a hybrid fund will give you a 24 per cent return."

Patrick pressed further. "That's good," he said, "but what about the losses?"

"Government securities will guarantee 8 per cent. With a high-risk fund, you'll lose, say, 60 per cent, but a hybrid fund will only lose 26 per cent or less due to profitable investment in government-backed securities like bonds and commercial papers."

"That would be better," Patrick said, "as it would only take three years for my money to double. And the stakes for the hybrid fund looks good, as the money I lose is nearly equal to the money I win, so the odds are one to one. However, the stock market seems to go higher and higher as the country develops, inflation sets in, and companies grow."

"Good!" Ben answered. "The other good thing is that you can buy as little as you can afford, with a minimum investment of RM100 per month."

"Well then," Patrick asked, "what are the magic words to becoming a millionaire from trust fund investment?"

"Investing in the right fund and making monthly investments, couple with dividend reinvestment, with the help of compounding will make you rich in no time."

"What is the risk then with trust fund investment?" Patrick asked.

"Recession and market crash, followed by devaluation of currency," Ben replied.

"Wouldn't every business be affected, more or less, by those situations as well?" Patrick said.

"Yes," Ben answered, "but we must always remember the cycles and the going concern of a business or in other words, will the business survive for our future generation to come."

"If a company is good, it will be a going concern, and it will follow the boom-bust-boom bust cycle."

"Yes," Ben replied with a chuckle. "Just keep your head when others are losing theirs – buy when everybody else is selling (during a market crash) and sell when everybody else is buying (during market bubbles)."

"Be a contrarian," Patrick posited.

"Yes," Ben answered. "I need a rest at the moment," he added. "Can we meet again next week?"

"Goodnight," Patrick said as he took his leave.

Both of them went off to sleep in their cosy beds, with Patrick dreaming of his first million and Ben dreaming of his first golden cheese.

Chapter 20

Broker

Patrick met Ben as usual in the attic on Saturday.

Ben asked Patrick, "What will someone who is falling down a cliff do?"

Patrick answered, "He will grab anything that he can lay his hand on."

Ben enquired further. "What will someone who is under heaps of debt do?"

Patrick answered, "Grab at any money or cash that he can lay his hands on."

"Is such a person more broke than you?" Ben asked.

"Yes," Patrick answered.

Ben continued, "That's why they are called broker."

"This means that a broker is someone who is more broke than you and would lay his hand on any money that he can get."

Ben nodded. "However," he added, "a broker must abide by the law or he or she will be sent to jail. So brokers give you legal advice and charge you commission on buying or selling a product, whether it is a car, house, or stock. They protect themselves by saying that they are not responsible for any losses accrued due to wrong advice."

"So, would becoming a broker, be a good career for someone who is just starting to work?"

"Yes," Ben told him. "The benefits are greater than the losses will be."

"What are the benefits, my master?" Patrick asked.

"You don't need any seed money. You will profit from spread or margin of the buyer and the seller (after matching them and gaining high commission)."

"Sounds good!" Patrick said. "I'm sure the requirements to be successful must be very high."

"To be a broker, you must be able to talk, find good deals, and convince others. Plus, you have to be good at closing deals. And if possible, you should get a professional qualification."

"Surely brokers need to have lots of knowledge and experience," said Patrick, "not to mention a good track record and proven trustworthiness."

"Yup," Ben answered.

"What would be the risks then?" Patrick wanted to know.

"Brokers must work round the clock," Ben answered. "They have to keep up with fussy and scrupulous buyers and sellers. It can be difficult to get a commission and it requires hard work. There is always the risk of rejection on unsuccessful deals, lack of customers, inability to close the deal and loss of commission due to non-payment by buyer or seller."

"So then, what's the good of becoming a broker?" Patrick asked.

"It's the fastest way to collect capital in order to be debt free or financially secure," Ben told him. "And if you are good, you can use other people's money (OPM) and other people's time (OPT) to work for your benefit."

Patrick asked, "So, as a broker I must hope not to be broker than my client?"

Ben reminded Patrick, "If you are looking for broker, next time, make sure that, when you want to buy shoes, you go to shoe dealer and when you want diamonds, you get them from a jewellery dealer and not vice versa."

"Yes, master!" Patrick replied.

Later, both of them said goodbye and went to sleep dreaming of how to make more money the next day.

Chapter 21

Franchise

Ben met Patrick again the following week. Ben asked Patrick whether he knew that there were business opportunities where he could make friends and make them as business partners – a situation in which he would share both the cost as well as the profit with his friends.

"No," Patrick said. "But judging from your question, I'd say this type of business surely exists."

"Yes," Ben answered. "We call it a franchise. A franchise," he explained, "is a business where you become the boss, get friends to become business partners, and make a profit together as buddies."

"Sounds good," Patrick answered.

Ben replied, "This is a fast way to grow a business. The business partners pool their cash to expand the business for the good of all of them."

Patrick replied, "In addition, such a business could expand to real estate. It's like what Ray Kroc said: 'We are not making hamburgers. We are making a real estate business.'" Patrick continued. "Wouldn't it be better if we were to be the master franchise?"

Ben agreed that it would. "But," he added, "We would need to have our own franchise chain, along with a recipe and the capacity to expand. Or we would need the opportunity and ability to get the master franchise from a reputed overseas franchise. However, master franchiser fees are very expensive and you need proper connections and channel that are difficult to get."

Patrick asked, "What about the basic requirements then?"

"Those include patents, trademarks, and recipe, as well as the capacity to conform to the rules and regulations of the company and country."

"It sounds like there would be high barrier of entry for a new company," Patricks said, adding, "and it allows us to develop own network for a franchiser system." He thought for a moment and asked, "What would be the magic words in franchising?"

"Star performer, marketing, and sales gimmicks," Ben replied.

"Then what are the difficulties of a franchising business?" Patrick asked.

"Franchisers need to work out of the office and sometimes around the clock. Getting a good start requires a good amount of resources or seed money in order to acquire the initial franchise, as well as proper patent and advertising."

"If we had all of this, the sky would be our limit?" Patrick asked.

Ben answered, "Yes, but make sure your franchise business is a tollgate surrounded by a swamp with Godzilla and an anaconda."

"Wow!" Patrick said. "Franchising is good for those entrepreneurs who can abide by the laws we have discussed."

"It's getting late," Ben said. "Let us retire to our beds."

"Goodnight," Patrick replied.

Ben answered, "You too!"

Chapter 22

Gambling

Patrick met Ben and asked, "Why do a lot of people like to gamble?"

"Greed," Ben answered. "That couple with fast buck mentality."

"Oh," said Patrick "But what is gambling really?"

"Gambling is a game of chance," Ben replied, "where the luckier person wins!"

"If this is the case," Patrick said, "gambling is bad!"

Ben agreed. "But," he added, "There are instant profits in gambling, for the lucky and those who have odds in their favour."

Patrick replied, "But I have seen horror stories where people go broke due to gambling."

"You're right," Ben said. "It does not pay to gamble! However, gambling can be a source of income for those who have luck (the main determining factor in whether gambling is a profitable endeavour), along with good gambling technique, proper knowledge, and practical experience."

"If this is the case, gambling is not right for me," Patrick replied. "But do you have any advice for those who like to gamble?"

"Gambling is fun when you win but a horror when you lose," Ben said. "The most important thing is to avoid losing your head when everybody else is losing theirs."

Chapter 23

Plantation

Patrick met Ben after coming home from a durian orchard near his house. Patrick gave Ben some durian and told him how nice the taste of the durian was. Ben was reluctant to try at first, but it tasted good after all.

Patrick claimed that the man in the orchard was "making a lot of money selling durian, and he is able to produce food for his fellow man."

"In addition to durian, crops like palm oil, flowers, water melon, and chillies are other good things to plant," replied Ben. "These crops are becoming more and more profitable with time. They give a constant return and farmers can grow them using organic farming methods, which promotes a healthy lifestyle and is a major catalyst for downstream industries, such as decoration, cordiality and the food business."

"If this is so good, why don't many people venture into plantation ownership?" Patrick asked.

"Owning a plantation requires a lot of hard work," Ben replied. "And there's risk involved. Finding land and dealing with long gestation periods for producing things like palm oil can prove difficult. In addition, such a venture requires a lot of capital and a great deal of manpower. Plantation owners have to deal with pest problems, finding good seedlings, and acquiring proper fertilizers. And it can be difficult to ensure that your growing methods are totally organic."

"I guess that's why my father is not keen on plantations," Patrick replied. "What are the basic requirements of a modern farmer?"

Ben answered, "You need to be an entrepreneur; you must be willing to learn and to fail, and you need to combine capital, land, natural resources, and labour."

"If this is the case," Patrick replied, "it is possible for farmers to be millionaires and, at the same time, contribute to mother earth."

"Yes," Ben told him. "But a modern farm must be based on organic farming and a healthy lifestyle to be successful and stay relevant in the future."

Patrick was yawning and bid farewell to Ben.

"Goodnight!" Ben said.

Chapter 24

Car Dealer

Patrick met Ben again the following Saturday. He had just come home in a Porsche driven by his friend's father. Patrick told Ben about his experience sitting in the Porsche.

Ben asked Patrick, "What is your friend's father vocation?"

"He's a car salesman," Patrick replied.

"Bingo," replied Ben. "My guess was correct! Do you want to know the advantages of being a car salesman?"

"Yup!" Patrick answered. "I would like to know."

"The rewards include access to fancy new cars, high margins or commissions, a high service incomes, and bonuses. Plus, you get to know a lot of people."

"The chance of driving impressive cars like my friend's dad's Porsche really thrills me," Patrick said. "But there are surely risks involved in this career."

Ben quickly listed the risks: "High bank loans, obsolete car stocks, damaged or faulty cars to repair or return, road tax and insurance, government regulations, clients' inability to pay high down payments or high instalments."

"Becoming a car salesman does not thrill me anymore," Patrick said. "I see that we would need a lot of capital, along with the ability of persuasion, and we would need to work round the clock."

"Still yet, do you want to know the basic requirements for becoming a car salesman?"

"Yeah!" Patrick replied.

"You must have knowledge about the types of cars and the current market prices for them. You must have experience and know a pool of buyers, sellers, insurance agents, adjustors, and government agencies," Ben told him.

"Oops, before I forget," Patrick added. "Is it a disadvantage that rules and regulation were set up to protect the consumer or government interests leading to negative returns?"

"Yes," Ben agreed. "But you must always remember to do something that you love and are passion about!"

As it was getting late, the two bids each other farewell, and each retired to his own bed.

Chapter 25

Collectors' Item

As usual, on Saturday, this time in the morning, Ben met Patrick. Ben showed Patrick his collection of badges. There were badges from countries like America, Australia, Great Britain, Nigeria, and Singapore. Patrick was surprised to see Ben's extensive collection. Ben told Patrick he got those badges, which were collectors' items from his visit to those country and exchanges he makes with his buddies.

Patrick asked Ben, "What is a collectors' item?"

"Something whereby there is a limited edition," Ben explained. "Examples include personal belonging like arts, stamps, coins, watches and amulets."

"Your collection looks extensive, but what are the rewards of becoming a collector?" Patrick asked.

"A high rate of return, for one," Ben answered, "which can be multiple times the initial investment. Other rewards include personal satisfaction, the enjoyment one gets from having a hobby and the fact that collecting, often encourages, one to study further. In addition, the items often hold sentimental value. And you can start with a small amount of capital, as collectors' items appreciate with time. Plus, some of them, like amulets, can be used for personal protection."

"What about the risk then?" asked Patrick.

Ben answered, "You'll need lots of capital if you'll be collecting expensive items. Then there's the chance of getting fake items; concerns about spoilage, theft, or damage; the need to repair damaged goods; and the need to acquire proper security and ensure good care of the item."

"What about the basic requirements to become a collector?" Patrick asked.

"Becoming a collector requires studying far and wide," Ben began. "You must be able to differentiate between the genuine and the fake. A genuine interest is important in order to get an original. It is wise to get a teacher and a catalogue as a guide. Plus, you want to accumulate capital to buy the items you're collecting; you'll need to match the buyer and seller markets and get samples from good and reputable services."

Patrick proceeded. "What about the essential knowledge that one needs?"

"As I said, it is essential to know how to tell the difference between fakes and the genuine items. You also need to understand the difference between low- and high-quality products. You need to know how to look for items that are a rarity (made by hand, for example, or limited editions from factories) and avoid collecting items that are in mass production. And you'll need to understand what is an item in pristine condition." Ben continued, "If you are willing to learn, you will be a rich and successful collector, and collectors will look for you to sell or buy their products, which can guarantee you a high return."

"What about a guru's advice?"

"As usual, buy in an area with lots of supply (a buyers' market) and sell in area with lots of demand (a sellers' market)," Ben told him.

After thoroughly reviewing Ben's badges, Patrick bid his mentor farewell and left the attic for the day.

Chapter 26

Writer

The school holiday was coming, and Patrick was getting ready to go for holiday. Patrick met Ben as usual on Saturday, before bidding his friend farewell. He would soon be leaving on his holiday to Paris.

Ben asked Patrick whether he knew that there was a job that would allow you to work even if you were away for holiday.

Patrick was surprised. "Really?" he asked.

"I'm talking about being a writer or an author to be exact," Ben explained.

"I think those who write fairy tales, health books, books on wealth management, scary stories and love novels must really profit big time," Patrick said.

"Yes," Ben agreed. "And on top of that high income (especially when sales are made in large quantities), authors get personal satisfaction, the ability to develop their creativity, and the opportunity to contribute to society. Writing can be part of the authors' hobby and writers can work anywhere, anytime, whenever they like."

"It seems to me the risk is minimal, and all we need is a good publisher and promotion," Patrick surmised.

"Yes!" Ben replied. "But the possibility of low sales is always a risk to consider."

"What is the make-up of a good writer?" Patrick asked.

"A zest to write, inborn talent, and interesting subject matter," Ben answered. "A writer must be good at storytelling and able to include both climax and anticlimax in the storyline."

"What are the things we need to be a successful writer?" Patrick asked.

"You'll you need to be able to dream and to write creatively. That plus ample time; proper resources (pen, paper, laptop, and printer); a good publisher; talent; and a touch of lady luck will make you a millionaire in no time." Ben continued, "Do what you like and are good at, and with the grace of god, success will be yours."

"What are the other advantages of a writer?" Patrick asked.

Ben answered, "Licensing and potential to enter ancillary businesses, like movies, restaurants, branding, and apparel."

"I imagine that, in addition, a writer must always have his own style and originality."

Ben nodded, and the two of them greet each other goodnight.

Chapter 27

Artist

Patrick came back from his vacation and told Ben about his family visit to see a comedy show in Paris. Patrick asked Ben, "Comedians fall under which category?"

"Artists," Ben answered, "which also include musicians, actors, decorators, sportsmen, and hosts of popular shows."

"What are the good things about becoming an artist?" Patrick asked.

"Personal satisfaction, wealth, popularity, high status, and the ability to contribute to society," Ben replied.

"Then are the risks are unpopularity and lack of a stable income?" Patrick guessed.

"You are right," Ben answered. "That's why there are so many aspiring actors on Broadway."

"What are the requirements then?" Patrick asked.

"A penchant to act, genius, or talent, all of which can be brought out under the tutelage of a successful teacher," Ben replied. "Plus knowledge, experience, creativity and willingness to try something new and unthinkable are important qualities."

Patrick asked, "What about your advice for young aspiring artist's then, wise mouse?"

"Do what you like and turn your hobby into your occupation, and success will be yours," Ben said.

With that, both of them retired to bed after saying goodbye.

Chapter 28

Administrator (Manager)

Patrick told Ben about his father going back to his job after being persuaded by his manager.

Ben asked Patrick, "What is a manager really?"

Patrick answered, "A person who manages others. Or in other words, a person who is good at manipulating people."

"Its like the food chain in employment," Ben offered. "We see the boss at the top, the manager in between, and the general worker at the bottom."

"Managers are in the employee group if I am not wrong," Patrick said, adding, "They trade their freedom for a temporary security."

"Yes," Ben answered. "Their security comes in the form of a fixed income, no loss to worry about, and a higher authority or guide to follow if something goes wrong. Plus, they enjoy a potential for high bonus during good sales periods."

"This only makes up for a temporary security," Patrick posited, "as they will be retrenched during recession, which will lead to late payment of income, loss of pay, and no social security contribution. And doesn't manager have to accumulate many years of experience and proper qualifications before getting their positions?"

Ben nodded. "In addition," he added, "you are waiting for pay and only barely surviving, as you are in the rat race and depend on cheese from day to day."

"Is there any advice you have for those in this category?" Patrick asked.

Ben replied, "The day for them to be rich is the day when they don't depend on a pay cheque anymore."

Chapter 29

Publisher/Director

Patrick's family decided to go to the cinema to watch a new show. They would be going the following day. Patrick was excited and told Ben about their plans. Ben told Patrick that the most important people behind the scene were the publisher and the director.

"Why?" Patrick asked.

"The director is like an entrepreneur. Directors join together multiple talented actors, gaining high income by way of multiplying effects," he answered, "Directors can also be brought to stardom. And publishers can apply for listings if they're successful, not to mention the reward of a tangible high income upon success."

"What are the risks then?" Patrick wanted to know.

"A movie or book flop leading to bankruptcy," Ben replied. "It's a high-risk, high-gain business."

"So the requirements would be a good director, coordinating actor, product manager, advertising, marketing, and sales?" Patrick asked.

"That's right!" Ben answered. "Always remember that, with the right touch, or the magic touch, we will be millionaires in the making."

Patrick bid Ben goodnight, and they promised to meet again the next week.

Chapter 30

Financial Consultant

It was early March when Patrick's father bought Patrick along to see his accountant, who would be preparing his father's income tax statement.

Patrick told Ben about his visit and asked Ben, "What is the job of an accountant?"

"An accountant or a financial consultant is someone who is well versed in accounting, finance, and the economy," Ben told him.

"The accounting firm looked very well decorated," Patrick said. "It must be very rewarding to be an accountant."

Ben replied, "You can be your own boss. You'll be well versed in the global economy, prudent at money management, and good at networking. And you'll be part of pulling in a high income for your partners. However," he added, "you'll need to have a high degree of qualification, specifically an accounting degree. In addition, being a successful accountant requires attaining quite a lot of experience (more than five years) and, in order to practice, you'll need a license."

"Are there other disadvantages?" Patrick asked.

"Yes," Ben assured him. "Accounting requires long working hours, stress management when facing unbalanced accounts, and overtime during the financial years end accounts. In addition, there are the potential loss of customers and a reputation to upkeep."

"It sounds good, but only for those who are willing to work hard to get the licenses to practice," Patrick replied.

The two told each other goodbye, as it was dinner time by then.

Chapter 31

Rental Businesses

Patrick discussed with Ben his visit to a hotel in Mount Titlis. It was a good hotel where people could rent a room for a day or two.

Ben told him, "This type of business falls under a category called rental business. Rental businesses include hotels and motels, service apartments, and car rentals."

"They roughly fall under the category of service industry," Patrick surmised, "where the customer is always right or, as the saying goes, the customer is the king."

Ben agreed. "The rewards include a high multiplier effect with other people's time, money, and labour and the potential for licensing and professional management," he said.

"What are the risks then?" Patrick asked.

"Lack of business due to poor marketing, sales, public relations, human resources, or product management," Ben answered.

"What about the essential requirements to be successful?" Patrick asked.

"To be successful in the rental business, you must be a good star performer, know how to implement good quality control, and have good disaster management skills," Ben began, "all whilst putting thy heart, thy soul, and thy life – aided with some luck – into the business. Do all this, and you will be a millionaire in no time."

Patrick thanked Ben, and they told each other good night before retiring to bed.

Chapter 32

Motivational Speaker

Patrick met Ben for their usual short discussion on making money. This Saturday, Ben asked Patrick to ponder whether there was a job where you made other people feel good and got paid for it.

Patrick thought a moment before answering, "Yes. That's the job of healthcare providers, like doctors and pharmacists."

"What about providing the feel-good factor for those who are well?" Ben prompted.

"Hmm," Patrick replied, considering the question. "Whatever it is, it sounds like a very great job," he finally said. "My wild guess is that it has something to do with advertising."

"Not quite," Ben answered. "The job I'm referring to is that of a motivational speaker. Or we can call it a motivational coach or guru."

"Some people seem to believe they are con men," said Patrick.

"What do you lose by feeling better about yourself – both financially and emotionally? Motivational gurus make us dare to dream of a better future. I believe both you and me would have been dead long ago if we didn't dream of a better future. As a result, we will be a better person. Pretending that our dreams will absolutely come true will make us happy people in the making. In other words," Ben concluded, "wish for the stars, but if you don't reach the stars, makes sure that you reach the moon."

"Does that mean motivational gurus are selling hopes?" Patrick enquired.

"Not only hopes but the essentials to a successful attitude," Ben replied, "which will bring you far in life – even farther than knowledge and skill can bring you."

"How?" Patrick asked.

"Remember our first motivational gurus," Ben prompted, "our parents?"

"Yes," Patrick said slowly. "Why?"

"Our parents were our first teachers," Ben explained. They are the ones who taught us motor skills and how to walk. If we didn't continue taking baby steps after failing when we were small, we would have been derelicts by now. In life, the determination of success starts with baby steps – where a journey of a thousand steps start with the first step, as expounded by Confucius."

"Oh, this sounds like a very good job," Patrick said. "Can you tell me more about the rewards of becoming one?"

"The rewards are that you can make your hobby of making people happy your vocation, you can contribute back to society and spread the feel-good factor around, and you can be well known," Ben told him. "Motivational gurus are able to communicate with many – via seminars, books, audiotape or videos. They make lots of new friends and do a lot of networking. Most importantly, they're able to see people change for the better in front of their eyes."

Patrick asked, "What about the risks then?"

"To be a motivational guru, you must be able to be persuasive talker and you must be willing to take the initiative. be lacking of time for self or family and you must be able to work around the clock. It can be a tiring job. You must be inclined to meet many people and to solve other people's problems. In addition, you won't have the security of a fixed income potential of failure is high."

Patrick enquired further, "Who are the type of people who will be very successful in this line of work?"

"A successful motivational guru is someone who reads far and wide, as lots of knowledge is the key to success," Ben answered. "He or she must have a good life experience (from self or friends) and be good at sharing parables – storytelling, in other words. Motivational gurus must be convincing, pleasant, able to work under stress, good at time management and good at team building."

"These are also good qualities adherent for those who work for the common good of the people, such as politicians and preacher," Patrick noted.

"If a person is working towards the common good, god will always be there to help him or her."

"Agreed," Patrick said, adding, "we can get a job that is satisfying and beneficial both personally and to our fellowman."

"A motivational speaker can become rich via seminars, studios, books, videos, road shows, personal coaching, or counselling," Ben said, "and through listing of his or her company."

"Most importantly," Patrick continued. "A guru can contribute to the financial wealth and emotional health of the community he or she lives in."

"That's what makes genuine motivational teachers continue to mold their fellow students," Ben said.

"Yes, master!" Patrick replied.

With that, Ben and Patrick bid each other farewell for the night.

Chapter 33

Inventor

It was Christmastime, and Patrick got a lot of toys this Christmas, as his rich aunt dropped by for a visit.

In the afternoon, Patrick met Ben again, as the two had become quite fond of each other. Patrick brought Ben a small gift. Ben, on the other hand, gave Patrick a small clip.

Patrick thanked Ben, even though he thought that the paper clip was cheap.

Ben told Patrick that a paper clip was a good investment because you could find a hundred of uses for paper clips.

Patrick agreed.

"Think of the toys you like, the sports equipments , the essential office supplies, the health food and the ergonomic furniture that exist today," Ben said. "Most of them were invented in the twenty-first century."

"Yes," Patrick replied, "I remember the craze for MASK toys, Transformers, Smurfs, Barbie dolls, and Hula-hoops. And of course, there's the daily need for essential items like staplers and liquid paper."

"Do you know that most of the inventors of those items are wealthy?" Ben asked.

Patrick nodded but kept quiet.

"They invented something, got it patented, and have the royalty working for them day and night," Ben said.

"It sounds like you're saying that an inventor does the hard work once, but enjoys the benefits repeatedly," Patrick offered.

"Exactly!" Ben answered. "And being an inventor means you can create and add something valuable to society. Plus you'll have a patent under your name; get a high residuals income and personal satisfaction, not to mention a continuous stream of income for your next of kin.

"Wow!" Patrick said. "Inventors can earn even after god makes a calling for them."

"But," Ben warned sharply, "don't reinvent the wheel, as doing so would be fruitless!"

Patrick nodded. "Other than that, what are the risks involved?" he asked after a moment.

"A lot of wasted time and effort," Ben replied. "And an inventor must be able to accept failure, along with the rejection of a product by the community. Other risks include marketing flops, safety issues, and lack of good ideas."

"Even if our invention were successful," Patrick added, "we would always face the chance of having no fixed income. Or we might work on something that wasn't the right investment at the time. Then there's the possibility of losing a patent or manipulation by other businessmen and the need to get a good marketer and advertiser."

Ben nodded. "That's why the way forward for an inventor is to patent the product even if it looks simple and cheap."

Patrick agreed and told Ben about the girl who patented the "Happy Birthday" song and made tons of money from it.

Ben was happy that Patrick was learning quickly and asked Patrick to apply what he had learned in his daily life whenever he had the chance to do so.

Patrick bid farewell to Ben whilst holding onto his paper clip dearly, as he knew that he had learned a very important lesson today.

Let us leave both of them for the time being and think about a good invention that might contribute to society.

Chapter 34

Fisheries/Husbandry

Patrick met Ben after coming home from a dinner at a well-known restaurant in town. Patrick told Ben about the nice scallops and oysters he'd had for dinner.

Ben asked Patrick whether he knew that produce from the sea would be the food of the rich in the future.

"Yes, because the pool of young fry and sea produce will be scarcer and scarcer due to over fishing," Patrick said.

"You're right," Ben answered. "That's why aquaculture is the way forward."

"Aquaculture involves the rearing of fish and seafood, such as crabs, prawn, lobsters, clams and sea cucumber; seaweed farming; and pearl culturing, right?" Patrick said.

"You are right again," Ben replied. "And the rewards of getting involved in this business include the ability to be your own boss, the possibility of a high return, and the ability to offer employment and fresh food to your friends. Plus, fish and seafood have a high export value as a commodity."

Patrick enquired, "What about the risks then?"

"The notion of dealing with livestock for food includes the risk of disease and working in an unnatural habitat. This work requires custom approval and the ability to acquire high-quality feedstocks, as well as a high level of hygiene; a large amount of start-up capital; and, most of all, a lot of aquaculture expertise. Then there is the risk of glut due to over rearing."

"What are the basic requirements for someone who is interested in this field?" Patrick asked.

"Knowledge, experience, skill, patience, and a lot of capital," Ben replied. "To be successful in this business, you must get quality feedstocks and be able to withstand long gestation periods. These are the real essentials of this business."

Patrick asked Ben to sum up aqua farming as a business.

"Aqua farming offers a high return commensurate with a high level of hard work," Ben told him.

Ben smiled at his friend. "I have told you what I know about earning money," he said. "However, our project is only half done, as you need to learn how to save, invest, and protect as well. This is because making money is easy for most people, but keeping it growing and protecting it is the difficult part for everybody.

"I am going on a trip around the world to visit my relatives and friends abroad. I will be coming back to see your progress later on. If you are good at earning money and I am satisfied with your progress, I will continue the second part and bring you on a trip to the Caribbean to meet "George, the tortoise king." I would like you to be good at the basics before I explain further.

"Always remember," Ben concluded, "that when the student is ready, the teacher will be there."

Patrick looked sad, as he had become fond of Ben. He was quiet for a while before finally sing softly, "So, you are leaving, my master?"

"No," Ben told him. "I am only going on vacation."

"Thank you, master. But please don't leave me alone, as I am only a small boy at the beginning of my quest for financial wealth," Patrick said.

"That you are, my student!" Ben replied. And he presented to Patrick a badge of courage that he had signed personally. "When you see the badge, it will represent me by your side, holding your hand as you journey along your path towards riches and success.

"If you fail," Ben added, "please have the courage to stand up. Remember the baby steps. Before I leave, I hope that the sun will shine before you on your path to financial wealth and the breeze will blow at you from behind."

Both of them cried as they hugged, bid each other farewell, and promised to meet again in the near future.

www.ingramcontent.com/pod-product-compliance
Lightning Source LLC
Chambersburg PA
CBHW030813180526
45163CB00003B/1271